Better Homes and Gardens®

SPECIAL PATCHWORK

© Copyright 1989 by Meredith Corporation, Des Moines, Iowa.
All Rights Reserved. Printed in the United States of America.
First Edition. First Printing.
Library of Congress Catalog Card Number: 89-60206
ISBN: 0-696-01850-0 (hard cover)
ISBN: 0-696-01851-9 (trade paperback)

BETTER HOMES AND GARDENS® BOOKS

Editor: Gerald M. Knox
Art Director: Ernest Shelton
Managing Editor: David A. Kirchner
Project Editors: James D. Blume, Marsha Jahns
Project Managers: Liz Anderson,
    Jennifer Speer Ramundt, Angela K. Renkoski

Crafts Editor: Sara Jane Treinen
Senior Crafts Editors: Beverly Rivers,
    Patricia M. Wilens
Associate Crafts Editor: Nancy J. Reames

Associate Art Directors: Neoma Thomas,
    Linda Ford Vermie, Randall Yontz
Assistant Art Directors: Lynda Haupert,
    Harijs Priekulis, Tom Wegner
Graphic Designers: Mary Schlueter Bendgen,
    Mike Burns, Brenda Lesch
Art Production: Director, John Berg;
    Associate, Joe Heuer;
    Office Manager, Michaela Lester

President, Book Group: Jeramy Lanigan
Vice President, Retail Marketing: Jamie L. Martin
Vice President, Administrative Services: Rick Rundall

BETTER HOMES AND GARDENS® MAGAZINE
President, Magazine Group: James A. Autry
Editorial Director: Doris Eby

MEREDITH CORPORATION OFFICERS
Chairman of the Executive Committee: E. T. Meredith III
Chairman of the Board: Robert A. Burnett
President: Jack D. Rehm

Special Patchwork
Photography Editor: Beverly Rivers
Contributing Editor: Elizabeth Porter
Editorial Project Manager: Angela K. Renkoski
Graphic Designer: Linda Ford Vermie
Contributing Graphic Designer: Patty Konecny
Electronic Text Processor: Paula Forest

Cover projects: See page 33.

CONTENTS

SEMINOLE PATCHWORK

♦ ♦ ♦

Deep in the Everglades of southern Florida, the Seminole Indians have created a unique form of patchwork to decorate their clothing. Rather than cutting and joining small, individual fabric squares, rectangles, or triangles, the Seminoles machine-stitch together narrow fabric strips. In this chapter, we've assembled projects to trim using this fast and simple method.

It takes almost no time at all to turn inexpensive purchased sweatshirts, *right,* into folk art wearables by adding vibrant bands of Seminole patchwork.

The red sweatshirt started as a basic raglan-sleeve shirt. The side seams and sleeve seams on the shirt were opened to simplify adding the bands.

The red, blue, turquoise, and yellow patchwork works equally well on the coordinating blue shorts. Stitch the shorts, and add the bands before the inner

leg seams are sewn, or machine-topstitch the bands to purchased shorts.

The yellow sweatshirt and green shorts sport identical patchwork squares joined into bands with different colored fabrics—green for the shirt and yellow for the shorts. To make bands on your projects look as if they really belong, choose at least one fabric for the patchwork that matches the background fabric as closely as possible.

Instructions for the projects in this chapter begin on page 12.

1 Cut fabric strips for Seminole patchwork across the fabric width so the strips are approximately 45 inches long.

Cut one 1½-inch-wide strip *each* from the turquoise and blue fabrics. Cut one 1¼-inch-wide strip from the yellow fabric.

To make a strip set, sew the strips together, lengthwise, taking ¼-inch seams and positioning the yellow strip in the center.

3 Draw placement lines on the right side of the patchwork band ¼ inch from the outer corners of the yellow squares.

For the edging strips, cut two 1-inch-wide strips from the yellow fabric and two ⅞-inch-wide strips from the red fabric.

Sew a red strip to a yellow strip, lengthwise. Press under ¼ inch on the yellow strip. Repeat to make a second edging strip set.

With right sides facing, sew an edging strip set to one side of the patchwork, aligning the red strip with the placement line.

2 Cut the strip set into 1¼-inch-wide segments.

Turning every other segment to alternate the colors, sew the segments together. Offset the strips so the top edge of the second yellow square is aligned with the bottom edge of the previous yellow square.

4 Using scissors or a ruler and a rotary cutter, trim the excess patchwork even with the raw edge of the edging strip.

Press seam allowances toward the edging strip set.

Repeat steps 3 and 4 to add the edging strip set to the opposite side of the band.

Quick-Cutting Patchwork Pieces

Use a rotary cutter for rapid and accurate cutting when your patchwork project requires lots of strips, squares, or rectangles. A rotary cutter resembles a pizza cutter but has a much sharper blade for cutting fabric. When used with a hard-edge ruler and a cutting mat, it cuts through multiple layers of fabric.

To cut a strip across the width of the fabric, fold the fabric *lengthwise* twice so it is folded with the selvage edges aligned with the fabric center fold. Lay the fabric on the cutting mat and then lay the ruler across the short edge, *perpendicular* to the fold. Most rulers recommended for use with rotary cutters have lines to help position the ruler.

Roll the cutter away from you along the ruler, exerting pressure on the cutter, to cut and straighten the fabric edge.

Moving across the fabric and aligning the ruler with the markings for the desired strip width, cut the required number of strips. After cutting every three or four strips, check to see that the cuts are perpendicular to the fold. If necessary, straighten the fabric edge before cutting more strips.

When cutting Seminole patchwork strip sets into segments, you can save time by cutting several matching strip sets at once. Or, fold a single strip set into fourths *lengthwise* to cut several segments simultaneously.

Stack multiple strip sets or fold a single strip set, aligning the seams and the raw edges. Using a rotary cutter and a ruler, cut through all of the layers. Most large rotary cutters will easily cut through up to eight layers of cotton broadcloth fabric; the smaller cutters will cut approximately four layers of fabric.

FIESTATIME

Come for:

Date:

Time:

Place:

Given

Inspired by an antique Seminole Indian doll, the doll *above* is dressed in traditional squaw clothing. The colorful yellow, purple, pink, and teal band on the skirt is stitched in a method similar to the log cabin piecing technique.

Multiple rows of tiny rickrack around the skirt hem and the cape add to the gay profusion of color typical in Seminole clothing.

Strings of tiny multi-colored beads dangle from her ears and loop around her neck to form jewelry.

Personalize your desktop with the handsome accessories at *left*.

Although the assembling of patchwork bands may appear complex and time consuming because the bands have so many tiny pieces, you can do it easily and quickly using a patchwork method developed by the Seminole Indians of Florida. Colorful strips of fabric are sewn together, then cut into pieced segments. When the segments are combined, wonderful designs emerge.

F or overnight guests, add a personal touch to your hospitality with these colorful bed and bath accessories. Trim sheets and pillowcases with bands of patchwork, *opposite,* and make a matching bedside caddy to complete the set.

Tuck the caddy between the mattress and springs, and fill some of the pockets with toiletries guests might have forgotten. In additional pockets, they can add personal items such as their glasses and favorite reading materials.

For the guest bathroom, embellish a set of coordinating towels and a washcloth, *above.* You can use the designs we've pictured or substitute any of the other designs in this chapter.

Red Sweatshirt And Blue Shorts

Shown on pages 4 and 7.

Seminole Design 1 measures approximately 1 inch wide between edging strips.

MATERIALS
Child's purchased red
  sweatshirt
Royal blue sport-weight fabric
  (yardage as specified in shorts
  pattern)
Yellow sewing thread
Rotary cutter, mat, and ruler
Commercial pattern for child's
  shorts
Notions for shorts as listed on
  pattern
Water-erasable marking pen

For the patchwork
½ yard of yellow fabric
⅓ yard of red fabric
¼ yard *each* of royal blue and
  turquoise fabrics

INSTRUCTIONS
To make Seminole Design 1
  Referring to the patchwork instructions on page 6 and to Drawing A, *right,* make four strip sets for Design 1.
  Stack strip sets and cut them into 1¼-inch-wide segments as shown in Drawing A. Join the segments into one long band as shown in Drawing B.
  Cut eight red and eight yellow edging strips. Join four red strips into a long edging strip; repeat for the remaining red strips and the yellow strips. To make an edging strip set, sew a long red strip to a long yellow strip; repeat. Press under ¼ inch on the yellow strips.
  Sew the red side of the edging strip sets to both sides of the patchwork band as shown in Drawing C. The long band should be approximately 144 inches.

To trim the sweatshirt
  Open each sleeve seam for approximately 6 inches from underarm. Extend the openings in the opposite direction an additional 6

inches by opening the side seam or by cutting the body of the sweatshirt if there are no side seams. The underarm openings should measure approximately 12 inches long.
  Using a water-erasable marking pen, mark a placement line across the sweatshirt front approximately 2 inches below the underarm. Measure the length of the placement line; cut a strip of patchwork this length.
  Mark a placement line around each sleeve approximately 2 inches below the underarm. Measure placement line and cut two strips of patchwork this length.
  Topstitch the bands to sweatshirt front and sleeves, aligning the upper edge of the bands with the placement lines.
  Taking ¼-inch seams, restitch sleeve seams. Continue the stitching to form side seams, tapering stitching at the end of the seam.

To make the shorts
  Following the pattern instructions, cut out the shorts from the blue fabric. If the pattern has side seams, sew the side seams.
  Mark placement lines for bands 2¼ inches from the bottom edge

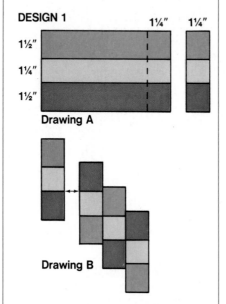

DESIGN 1

1¼"   1¼"

1½"
1¼"
1½"

Drawing A

Drawing B

Seam lines

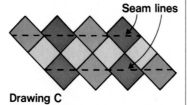

Drawing C

of each leg. Measure the length of the placement line; cut two patchwork strips this measurement.
  Pin the wrong side of a Seminole band to the right side of one leg, aligning the lower band edge with the placement line. Using matching thread, topstitch along both long sides of the band. Repeat for the other leg.
  Complete the shorts as directed in the pattern instructions.

Yellow Sweatshirt And Green Shorts

Shown on pages 4–5.

Seminole Design 2 measures approximately 3 inches wide between edging strips.

MATERIALS
Child's purchased 3-button
  yellow sweatshirt
Royal blue sewing thread
Rotary cutter, mat, and ruler
Pattern for child's shorts
Notions for shorts as listed on
  pattern
Green sport-weight fabric
  (yardage as specified on shorts
  pattern)
Water-erasable marking pen

For the patchwork
½ yard of yellow fabric
⅛ yard of purple fabric
¼ yard *each* of royal blue and
  green fabric

INSTRUCTIONS
  Refer to the instructions on pages 6 and 7 for general instructions on Seminole patchwork.
  Use a rotary cutter and ruler to cut all strips across the fabric width so the strips are approximately 45 inches long.

To make Seminole Design 2
  You will need two different strip sets to make this design.

  TO MAKE STRIP SET 1: Cut two ¾-inch-wide strips from the yellow fabric.
  Cut two 1½-inch-wide strips *each* from the blue and the purple fabrics.

Sew the strips together in the order shown in Drawing A, *below right.* Press the seam allowances toward the center strip. Repeat to make one more strip set.

Cut these strip sets into 1½-inch-wide segments. For faster cutting, you can stack the strip sets and cut both layers simultaneously with a rotary cutter. Set these segments aside.

TO MAKE STRIP SET 2: Cut two 1½-inch-wide strips from the yellow fabric.

From the green fabric, cut one ¾-inch-wide strip.

Sew the strips together in the order shown in Drawing B, *right.* Press the seams away from the center strip.

Cut Strip Set 2 into ¾-inch-wide segments.

TO MAKE PIECED SQUARES: Referring to Drawing C, *right,* sew together two segments from Strip Set 1 and one segment from Strip Set 2, turning the Strip Set 1 segments so the colors alternate.

Make the individual squares as shown, but *do not* join the squares to each other.

To trim the yellow sweatshirt
TO MAKE BAND: From the green fabric, cut two 2¾-inch-wide strips. Cut the strips into 4½-inch-long segments.

Referring to Drawing D, *below,* sew pieced squares and green segments together, starting and ending with a green segment. For a size Medium child's sweatshirt,

you will need approximately five or six of the pieced squares. Set the remaining squares aside to make the shorts.

Referring to Drawing D, cut diagonally through the green segments, positioning diagonal cuts ½ inch from pieced squares.

Join the pieces into one long strip, offsetting pieces as shown in Drawing E, *below.* Check strip length to be sure it will fit across the sweatshirt chest. Add more squares, if necessary.

TO ADD EDGING STRIPS: From the blue fabric, cut two 1-inch-wide edging strips.

With a water-erasable marking pen, mark placement lines on the patchwork band ½ inch from outer corners of the pieced squares.

DESIGN 2

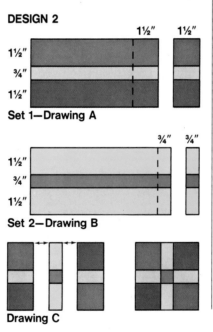

Set 1—Drawing A

Set 2—Drawing B

Drawing C

Pin edging strips to patchwork, aligning raw edge of edging strips with placement lines. Sew edging strips to patchwork. Trim excess patchwork. Turn under ¼ inch along the long raw edge of both edging strips.

The band, including the edging strips, should measure approximately 4¼ inches wide.

ASSEMBLY: Mark a placement line across the sweatshirt front below the front placket. Pin the wrong side of the Seminole band to the right side of the sweatshirt front, aligning the top band edge with the placement line. Trim band length and turn under ¼ inch on the band ends. Topstitch band to sweatshirt.

To make the shorts
TO MAKE BAND: From the yellow fabric, cut two 2¾-inch-wide strips. From the blue fabric, cut two 1-inch-wide edging strips.

Substituting yellow strips for green strips, follow instructions, *left,* for sweatshirt to make a long patchwork band using remaining pieced squares. Add the blue edging strips to the patchwork.

Following the pattern instructions, cut out the shorts. If the pattern has side seams, sew the side seams.

On each leg, mark a placement line 2¼ inches up from the bottom edge. Cut two patchwork pieces the length of the placement line.

continued

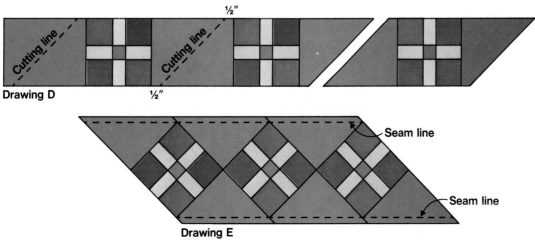

Drawing D

Drawing E

Seam line

Seam line

ASSEMBLY: Pin the wrong side of a Seminole band to the right side of one leg, aligning the lower band edge with the placement line. Using matching thread, machine-topstitch along both long sides of the band.

Repeat to sew the band to the other leg.

Complete the shorts as directed in the pattern instructions.

Address Book

Shown on page 8.

The finished address book is 6½x7½ inches.

Seminole Design 3 is approximately 1¾ inches wide between the edging strips; Design 4 is approximately ¾ inch wide.

MATERIALS

½ yard of navy fabric
¼ yard of muslin
Scraps of dark teal, turquoise, and tan fabrics for edging strips
Rotary cutter, mat, and ruler
Address book, approximately 6½x7½ inches.
¼ yard of polyester fleece

For the patchwork

⅛ yard *each* of rose, yellow, light teal, lavender, blue, and rust fabrics
¼ yard of peach fabric

INSTRUCTIONS

Note: The instructions are written to custom-cover any book of similar size.

To make Seminole Design 3

Cut one 1-inch-wide strip each from the peach, rose, yellow, light teal, lavender, and blue fabrics.

To make this strip set, sew the strips together in the order shown in Drawing A, *right.* Press seams to one side.

Cut the strip set into 1-inch-wide segments.

Referring to Drawing B, *right,* sew the segments together into a long band, offsetting each segment by one square. Press the seams to one side.

To make Seminole Design 4

Cut one 1¼-inch-wide and one ¾-inch-wide strip *each* from the rust and peach fabrics.

To make Strip Set 1, sew a wide rust strip to a narrow peach strip as shown in Drawing A, *opposite.* Press seam allowances toward the rust strip. Make one more strip set from wide rust and narrow peach strips.

Repeat these instructions, using the wide peach strip and the narrow rust strip to make one Strip Set 2.

Cut both strip sets into ¾-inch-wide segments. For faster cutting, you can stack the strip sets and cut the layers simultaneously with a rotary cutter.

Referring to Drawing B, *opposite,* sew the Strip Set 1 segments together into two long strips. Sew the Strip Set 2 segments together into one long strip.

Sew the three pieced strips together with the Strip Set 2 band

DESIGN 3

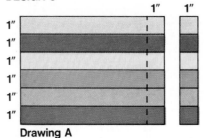

Drawing A

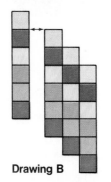

Drawing B

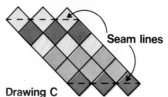

Drawing C

in the center, offsetting the segments so small rust squares are centered between long rust strips as shown in Drawing C, *opposite.* Press seams to one side.

To make the book cover

To make a pattern for the book cover, open the book and trace around cover onto a piece of paper. Add ¼ inch for seams around pattern. Use the pattern to cut a piece of muslin to use as the foundation for the patchwork.

From the dark teal, turquoise, navy, and tan fabrics, cut strips that vary from ¾ to 1¼ inches wide for the edging strips.

Pin the wrong side of a band of Design 3 diagonally across the lower-right corner of the muslin; trim excess band that extends beyond the muslin foundation.

Sew a dark teal edging strip, right sides facing, along the diagonal edge of the band. The dashed lines on Drawing C, *below left,* indicate approximate placement for edging strips. Trim excess. Open out the edging strip and add a strip of another color.

In a similar manner, alternately add edging strips and bands of Design 3 and Design 4 until the muslin is covered.

Compare the patchwork cover to the paper pattern to see that the cover is the correct size. If necessary, add navy edging strips along the outer edges to achieve the needed size.

ASSEMBLY: Use the paper pattern to cut a piece of fleece and a lining piece from the navy fabric. Baste fleece to the wrong side of the patchwork cover.

For the flaps, cut two navy blue pieces that are approximately 6 inches wide and the height of the pattern. On one long side of *each* flap piece, press under ¼ inch twice; machine-hem. With right sides facing and raw edges even, sew the flaps to the ends of cover.

Pin right side of lining atop wrong sides of flaps. Sew around the cover, leaving an opening for turning. Clip corners, turn, and press; sew the opening closed. Slip cover of book into flaps.

Paperweight

Shown on page 9.

The finished paperweight is 3x5 inches.

MATERIALS
3½-inch-long piece of Seminole Design 3 band (see the Instructions under Address Book on page 14)
3½x5½-inch rectangle of navy fabric (lining)
Scraps of assorted colors for edging strips
Peach embroidery floss
Unpopped popcorn

INSTRUCTIONS
Sew edging strips to the patchwork band to form a 3½x5½-inch rectangle. With right sides facing, sew the front and lining together, leaving an opening for turning. Clip corners and turn right side out. Fill with popcorn kernels and stitch opening closed.

To make one tassel, cut 12 pieces of embroidery floss, each 3 inches long; fold pieces in half. Approximately ¼ inch from the fold, secure pieces by wrapping with floss. Tack a tassel to one corner. Repeat to make a tassel for the remaining corners.

DESIGN 4

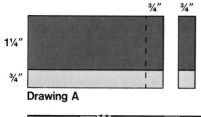

Drawing A

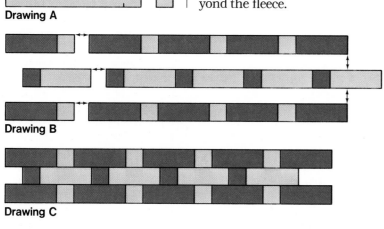

Drawing B

Drawing C

Pencil Holder

Shown on page 8.

The pencil holder is 3 inches in diameter and 4½ inches high.

MATERIALS
8-inch-long pieces *each* of Seminole Design 3 and Design 4 bands (see Instructions for Address Book on page 14)
¼ yard *each* of navy fabric and polyester fleece
Scraps of assorted colors for edging strips
10-inch-long piece of flexible magnetic tape
Tin can, approximately 3 inches in diameter and 4½ inches high
Paper and pencil

INSTRUCTIONS
To make the pattern for the base, trace around the bottom of the can onto paper. To make the pattern for the cover, wrap a piece of paper around the can; mark the top and bottom of the can and the spot where the paper overlaps. Cut out the pattern pieces, adding ¼-inch seam allowances.

From the navy fabric, cut a rectangle the length of the cover pattern and 3½ inches wide for the lining. Cut one circle for the base.

Using the cover pattern, cut one rectangle from fleece.

Pin the wrong side of a band of Design 3 diagonally across the lower-right corner of the fleece; trim excess band that extends beyond the fleece.

Place a dark teal edging strip, right sides facing, along the diagonal edge of the band; sew the edging strip to the patchwork, trimming excess. Open out the edging strip and add a strip of another color.

In a similar manner, alternately add edging strips and bands of Design 3 and Design 4 until the fleece is covered.

Check to see that the patchwork cover is the same size as the paper pattern. If necessary, add navy blue edging strips along outer edges to achieve correct size.

ASSEMBLY: Fold under ¼ inch twice along one long edge of the 3½-inch-wide lining rectangle; machine-hem.

With right sides facing, sew the lining piece to the top edge of the patchwork rectangle. Stitch the side seam of the patchwork and lining in one long seam, forming a tube. Stitch the round bottom piece to the end of the patchwork that is opposite the lining. Clip and turn right side out.

Fit the can into the cover; tuck the lining to the inside. Adjust the fit of the cover as necessary.

Cut a length of magnetic tape the circumference of the inside of the can. Wrap the magnetic tape over the lining on the inside of the can to hold the lining in place.

Desk Blotter Cover

Shown on pages 8–9.

Finished cover is approximately 16½x22 inches.

MATERIALS
1 yard of navy fabric
Scraps of dark teal, turquoise, rust, and tan fabrics
Rotary cutter, mat, and ruler
Purchased blotter paper, approximately 16x22 inches

For the patchwork
⅛ yard *each* of peach, rose, yellow, light teal, lavender, and blue fabrics
¼ yard of peach fabric

continued

INSTRUCTIONS

The patchwork for the blotter cover is a pyramidlike variation of Seminole Design 3.

Note: The instructions are written to custom-cover any blotter paper of similar size.

To make the Design 3 variation

To cut the strips, refer to the instructions to make Seminole Design 3 on page 14.

Sew the strip set, omitting the peach strip. Cut the strip set into 1-inch-wide segments, but *do not* sew the segments into a band.

From the peach strip, cut two segments *each* in the following lengths: 1 inch, 2 inches, 3 inches, 4 inches, and 5 inches.

To make one pyramidlike formation, remove the rose square from one segment. Referring to the photograph on page 8, join the shortened segment to a complete segment. Sew together pairs of segments, placing progressively longer peach strips between segments. Join segments.

From the dark teal, turquoise, rust, and tan fabrics, cut edging strips that vary from ¾ to 1¼ inches wide. Cut a 4-inch-wide edging strip from the navy fabric.

Add multicolored edging strips to outer edges along blue squares; sew navy edging strips to ends. Repeat to make a patchwork section for the other side.

To make the blotter cover

Using the blotter paper as a pattern, cut two rectangles from the navy fabric, adding ¼-inch seam allowances. Cut two rectangles for the flap linings that are 3½ inches wide and ½ inch longer than the width of the paper.

TO MAKE ONE FLAP: Using a flap lining piece as a pattern, trim excess edging strips on the patchwork panels.

Pin a patchwork panel to a flap lining piece with right sides facing and raw edges matching. Sew along the side with the single rose square. Turn right side out and press seam. Repeat to make a flap for the other side.

ASSEMBLY: Baste a flap to each end of the blotter rectangle, right sides facing. Place the rectangle atop the second rectangle, right sides facing. Sew around the cover, leaving an opening for turning. Clip, turn, and stitch the opening closed.

Slip the cover over the ends of the blotter paper.

Seminole Doll

Shown on page 9.

Finished doll is 10 inches tall.

Seminole Design 5 is approximately 2¾ inches wide between the edging strips.

MATERIALS
½ yard of brown fabric
Black, red, and white
  embroidery floss
Multicolored seed beads
Polyester fiberfill
Unpopped popcorn

For the clothing
¼ yard *each* of yellow, orange,
  pink, purple, teal, green, red,
  and black fabrics
Scrap of blue fabric
3x5-inch recipe card
Baby rickrack in the following
  colors: navy, black, light
  green, and red

INSTRUCTIONS
To make the doll

Trace the patterns for the doll and the doll clothing, *opposite*, matching the AB lines to complete the doll body. Patterns are finished size; add ¼-inch seam allowances when cutting the pieces from fabric.

From the brown fabric, cut two of the doll body. Transfer the facial details to the doll front. Using embroidery floss, embroider eyes and a mouth on the doll face.

With right sides facing and taking ¼-inch seams, sew the body pieces together, leaving the bottom open. Clip seams and turn.

Firmly stuff the head and the upper 4 to 5 inches of the torso with polyester fiberfill.

Stuff the lower torso with popcorn to add weight to the doll. Turn under ¼ inch along the bottom edge. Gather bottom edge; stitch the opening closed.

To make Seminole Design 5

You will need two different strip sets to make this design.

TO MAKE STRIP SET 1: Cut one 1-inch-wide strip *each* from pink, yellow, and purple fabrics.

Sew the strips together in the order shown in Drawing A on page 18. Press seam allowances all in one direction. Cut the strip set into 1-inch-wide segments.

TO MAKE STRIP SET 2: Cut a 1½-inch-wide strip from the yellow fabric; cut a 1-inch-wide strip from the purple fabric.

Sew the strips together in the order shown in Drawing B on page 18. Press seam allowances all in one direction. Cut the strip into 1-inch-wide segments.

TO MAKE PIECED SQUARES: Cut a 2-inch-wide strip from purple fabric. Cut the strip into 1-inch-wide segments.

Referring to Drawing C on page 18, sew together purple segments and segments of Strip Set 1 and Strip Set 2.

Make the individual squares as shown, but *do not* join squares to each other.

TO MAKE BAND: From the teal fabric, cut two 3-inch-wide strips. Cut each of the strips into 2-inch-wide segments.

From the remaining teal fabric, cut two 1-inch-wide strips. Cut strips into 7-inch-long segments.

Referring to Drawing D on page 18, stitch a 2x3-inch teal segment to opposite sides of the pieced squares. Alternating the pieced squares and 7-inch-long teal segments, sew the pieces together into a long strip.

continued

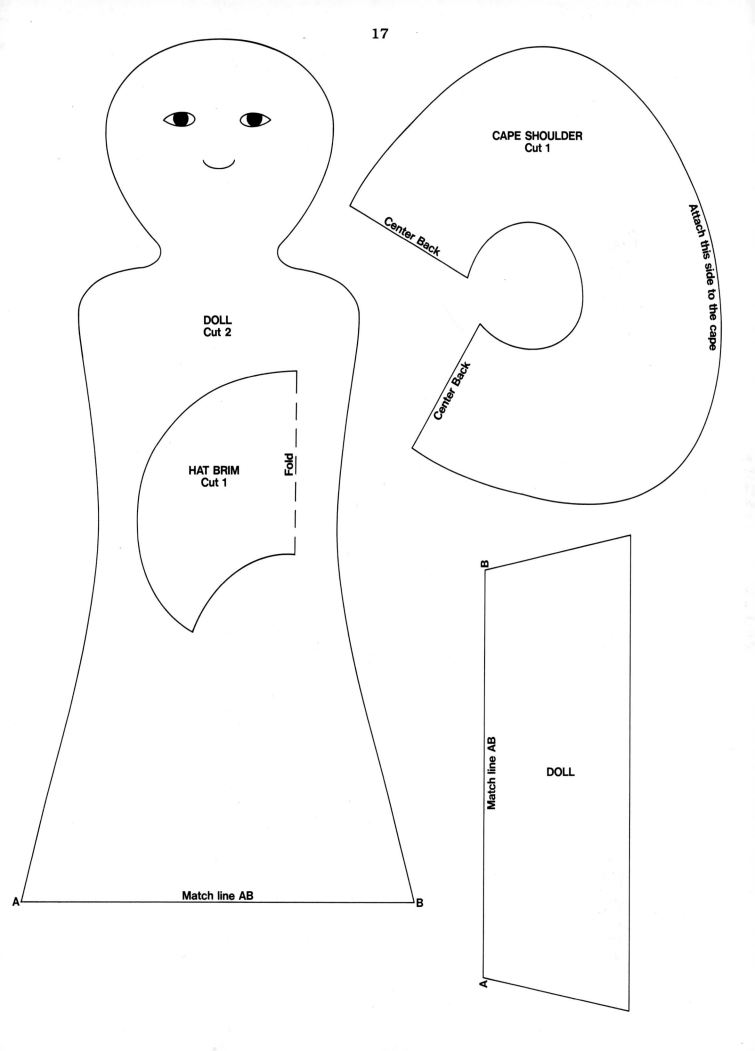

CAPE SHOULDER
Cut 1

Center Back

Attach this side to the cape

Center Back

DOLL
Cut 2

HAT BRIM
Cut 1

Fold

B

Match line AB

DOLL

A

Match line AB

A   B

Mark placement guidelines for the edging strips on the right side of the patchwork band to each side of pieced squares, spacing the guidelines 3 inches apart.

To make the clothing

TO MAKE SKIRT: Cut 36-inch-long edging strips for the skirt as follows: Cut one 1¾-inch-wide strip from the red fabric. Cut one 1¼-inch-wide strip from the purple fabric. Cut one 2½-inch-wide strip from the orange fabric.

Press the orange strip in half so it is 1¼ inches wide. Matching the raw edges of the edging strip to the lower guideline, sew the strip to the band, finishing the lower skirt edge. Trim the excess patchwork. Press seams toward the edging strip.

Sew the red edging strip to the top edge of the patchwork band; trim excess patchwork and press.

Sew the purple edging strip to the red strip. Turn under and narrowly hem the top edge of the purple strip.

Stitch a row of red and a row of black rickrack to the orange strip.

DESIGN 5

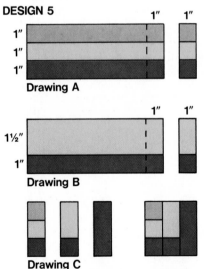

Drawing A

Drawing B

Drawing C

Sew a row of green rickrack to the red strip.

Trim skirt rectangle so it is approximately 6½x36 inches. Sew the center back seam. Gather the top edge of the skirt. Slip the skirt on the doll; draw up and fasten the gathered edge to fit snugly around the doll's waist.

TO MAKE CAPE: Cut 26-inch-long strips as follows: one 2-inch-wide green strip, one 2¼-inch-wide pink strip, and one 1½-inch-wide yellow strip.

Fold the green strip in half so it is 1 inch wide. Matching raw edges, sew the pink strip to the green strip. Sew the yellow strip to the pink strip.

Sew red rickrack to the green strip. Sew light green and black rickrack to the pink strip. Sew navy rickrack to the yellow strip.

Trim the rectangle so it is approximately 3½x25 inches.

From the blue fabric scrap, cut one shoulder piece. Gather the yellow edge of the cape rectangle; sew to the outer edge of the shoulder piece.

Sew the center back seam, leaving the upper edge open to slip the cape over the doll's head. Slip the cape on the doll; finish the center back seam. Gather blue shoulder piece to fit snugly around the doll's neck.

TO MAKE HAT: From the recipe card, cut the hat brim.

From the black fabric, cut a 5x8-inch rectangle.

Fold the fabric over the brim. Pin the hat on the doll's head. Form small pleats in the black fabric; tack the raw edges to the sides and back of the doll's neck. Add additional stitches as needed to secure the hat; remove pins.

FINISHING: String a long strand of beads. Wrap the beads loosely around the doll's neck five or six times.

To form earrings, stitch loops of beads to sides of the doll's head.

Trimmed Sheet and Pillowcases

Shown on page 11.

Seminole Design 6 is approximately 3 inches wide between the edging strips.

MATERIALS
Flat sheet for a double bed and a pair of pillowcases
Rotary cutter, mat, and ruler
Water-erasable marking pen

For the patchwork
⅝ yard of green and white print fabric
¼ yard of pink print fabric
½ yard of dark green fabric
½ yard of rose fabric

INSTRUCTIONS
Preshrink all fabrics, the sheet, and the pillowcases.

To make Seminole Design 6
TO MAKE BAND: Cut two 3-inch-wide strips from the white print fabric.

From the pink print fabric, cut two 1-inch-wide strips.

From the dark green fabric, cut one 2-inch-wide and two 3-inch-wide strips.

From the rose fabric, cut four 1-inch-wide strips. Cut rose strips into 7½-inch-long segments.

To make a strip set, sew the strips together in the order shown in Drawing A, *opposite*. Press seams in one direction.

Cut the strip set into 2-inch-wide segments.

Sew a rose segment to one side of all pieced segments as shown in Drawing B, *opposite*.

Referring to Drawing B, join the segments, offsetting each segment so the top pink print strip is aligned with the bottom pink

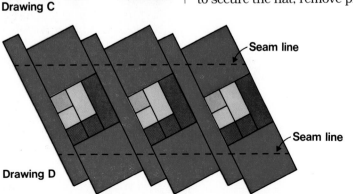

Drawing D

Seam line

Seam line

print strip of the previous segment. Press the seams to one side.

Note: One 45-inch strip set produces a band approximately 65 inches long.

Repeat instructions, above, to make a total of three sets of Design 6. For faster cutting, you can stack strip sets and cut the layers simultaneously with a rotary cutter and a heavy plastic ruler.

If necessary, cut additional rose segments, then join all segments into one long band. The long band should measure approximately 195 inches.

TO ADD EDGING STRIPS: From the dark green fabric, cut ten 1-inch-wide strips.

Sew five green strips together into one long edging strip. Press the long strip in half lengthwise, with wrong sides facing, so it is ½ inch wide. Repeat for the remaining five green strips.

Sew the edging strips to both sides of the band. Seams should be approximately ½ inch from outer points of green squares.

DESIGN 6

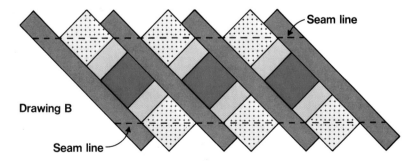

Drawing A

Drawing B

Seam line

Press the seams and trim the excess patchwork.

To trim the sheet

Note: Plan the placement of the Seminole band so it will either cover any decorative trim on the sheet hem or coordinate with it.

Using a water-erasable marking pen, mark a placement line across the width of the sheet, 1½ inches from the hem fold. Cut a piece of patchwork ½ inch longer than the width of the sheet.

Pin the wrong side of the band to the right side of the sheet, aligning the top edge of the band with the placement line.

Turn under the ends of the band so they are even with sheet. Using matching thread, topstitch the band to the sheet.

To trim the pillowcases

Mark a placement line around one pillowcase 1½ inches from the hem fold. Cut a piece of patchwork 1 inch longer than placement line.

Beginning at side seam on pillowcase, pin wrong side of band to right side of pillowcase, aligning the outer edge of the band with the placement line.

Trim the end of the band ¼ inch longer than is needed to allow for finishing.

Turn under end of the band to cover the beginning edge. Machine-topstitch the band to the pillowcase. Hand slip-stitch the end of the band over the beginning edge.

Repeat the instructions to add trim to the second pillowcase.

Reading Caddy

Shown on page 11.

Finished reading caddy is approximately 9½x13½ inches.

Seminole Design 1 is approximately 1 inch wide between the edging strips.

MATERIALS
1½ yards of green and white print fabric
7x12-inch piece of cardboard
16x20-inch piece of polyester fleece
Rotary cutter, ruler, and mat
Rose sewing thread

For the patchwork
¾ yard of light green fabric
⅛ yard *each* of pink print, dark green, green and white print, and rose fabrics

INSTRUCTIONS
Seminole Design 1 was used on the Reading Caddy shown in the photograph on page 11. If desired, you can substitute a different Seminole design of similar width for Design 1.

To make Design 1, refer to the instructions on page 12. Substitute light green fabric for turquoise fabric, dark green fabric for royal blue fabric, and pink print fabric for yellow fabric. Make one strip set; cut into segments. When joining segments, *do not* turn segments to alternate the colors.

TO ADD EDGING STRIPS: From the rose fabric, cut two 1-inch-wide strips. Press the strips in half lengthwise so they are ½ inch wide.

Sew the folded edging strips to the patchwork band as directed for Design 1.

Cut the band into two 15-inch-long pieces.

To make the caddy
TO CUT PIECES: From green and white print fabric, cut two 15x19-inch rectangles for main portion of caddy.

continued

From the green and white fabric, cut pockets as follows: For the front pockets, cut one 15x18-inch rectangle and one 12½x15-inch rectangle. For back pocket, cut one 9x13-inch rectangle.

From the light green fabric, cut two 9½x15-inch rectangles for the contrasting pocket and lining.

Trim the top corners at an angle along one 15-inch side of each light green rectangle. To mark the trim line, mark a spot 5 inches in from each outer edge, leaving 5 inches in the center. Mark a spot 2½ inches down from the top edge on each side. Connect the marks, forming a triangle on each side. Trim away the triangles from the outer corners.

TO MAKE FRONT POCKETS: To make the contrasting pocket, pin the light green pocket and the pocket lining pieces together with right sides facing and raw edges matching. Stitch along the angled edges. Turn right side out; press.

To make the smaller pocket, fold the 12½x15-inch green and white print rectangle in half so it is 6¼ inches wide.

Pin the wrong side of a Seminole piece to the print pocket, aligning the edge of the Seminole piece with the folded pocket edge. Topstitch along both sides of Seminole band.

Pin the smaller pocket atop the contrasting pocket. Stitch center of smaller pocket to divide it into two pockets and to attach it to the contrasting pocket.

To form the large pocket, fold the 15x18-inch rectangle in half, wrong sides facing, so it is 9 inches wide.

Pin the wrong side of a strip of Seminole patchwork to the pocket, aligning the edge of the band with the folded pocket edge. Topstitch along the top edge. *Do not* stitch the bottom edge.

Position the contrasting pocket so the 5-inch-wide section is centered under the lower edge of the Seminole band. Topstitch lower edge of band to pocket, catching the top edge of the contrasting pocket in the stitching and securing it to the large pocket.

ASSEMBLY: To make the quilted base, sandwich the fleece between two 15x19-inch green and white print rectangles. Machine-quilt in lengthwise rows spaced approximately 1 inch apart. Trim excess batting.

Pin the layered pockets to one end of the caddy front, aligning the lower pocket edges with the end of the caddy. Baste the pockets to the caddy along the sides and bottom.

Machine-stitch a narrow hem along one long edge of the 9x13-inch back pocket. Pin the wrong side of the pocket to the back of the caddy at the end without front pockets. Baste the pocket to the caddy along the sides and bottom.

Trim the corners of the caddy to round them slightly.

FINISHING: From the remaining green and white print fabric, cut approximately 60 inches of 2½-inch-wide bias binding. Fold the binding in half so it is 1¼ inches wide.

Sew the binding around the caddy. Turn the folded edge of the binding to the caddy back and stitch in place.

Trimmed Towels

Shown on page 10.

Seminole Design 7, for the pink towels, is 1½ inches wide between edging strips.

Seminole Design 8, for the green towels, is 2½ inches wide between the edging strips.

MATERIALS
For both towel sets
Rotary cutter, ruler, and mat
Dark green sewing thread

For the pink towels
Set of towels, including washcloth, hand towel (16x29 inches), and bath towel (25x50 inches)
¼ yard *each* of dark green, pink print, and white print fabrics

For the green towels
Set of towels, including washcloth, hand towel (16x29 inches), and bath towel (25x50 inches)
⅓ yard of dark green fabric
¼ yard of light green fabric
¼ yard of pink print fabric

INSTRUCTIONS
Preshrink the towels and the fabrics for the patchwork.

Design 7 was used on the pink towels shown in the photograph on page 10, and Design 8 was used on the green set.

To make Seminole Design 7
Cut one 2-inch-wide strip *each* from the white and pink fabrics.

DESIGN 7

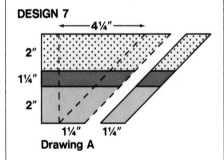

Drawing A

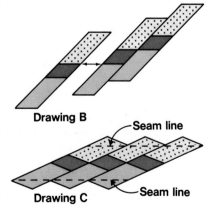

Drawing B

Drawing C

Cut one 1¼-inch-wide strip from the dark green fabric.

To make a strip set, sew strips together in the order shown in Drawing A, *opposite*. Press seam allowances toward white fabric.

Using a rotary cutter and ruler, cut the strip set at a 45-degree angle into 1¼-inch-wide segments.

If your ruler does not have markings for 45-degree-angle cuts, mark a vertical line at one end of the strip set. Mark a point along the top edge of the strip set, 4¼ inches from the vertical line. Mark a diagonal line from the top point to the base of the vertical line. Cut along the diagonal line. Cut additional segments parallel to the first diagonal cut.

Join the segments, offsetting the segments as shown in Drawing B, *opposite*. The lower edge of the second green piece should be aligned with the top edge of the first green piece. Join all of the segments in this manner.

The band should be approximately 44 inches long.

TO ADD EDGING STRIPS: Cut one ⅞-inch-wide strip *each* from the pink print fabric and the white print fabric.

Cut two 1½-inch-wide strips from the dark green fabric. With wrong sides facing, press the green strips in half, so they are ¾ inch wide.

Matching the raw edges, stitch a green strip to a white strip. Press seams toward green strip.

Stitch the second green strip to the pink strip. Press the seam allowances toward the green strip.

Sew the pink and green edging strip to the white portion of the patchwork ½ inch below the bottom edge of the green diamonds. The dashed lines on Drawing C indicate the approximate edging strip placement. Trim the excess patchwork, leaving approximately ¼-inch seam allowances.

Repeat to add the white and green edging strips to the pink side of the patchwork.

To make Seminole Design 8

Cut two 2-inch-wide strips *each* from the dark green fabric and the light green fabric.

From the pink fabric, cut two 1¼-inch-wide strips.

To make a strip set, sew the strips together in the order shown in Drawing A, *right*. Press seam allowances toward the dark green fabric. Repeat to make a second strip set.

Aligning matching strips, stack the two strip sets with *wrong* sides facing. Cutting both strip sets simultaneously, cut the strip sets at a 45-degree angle into 1¼-inch-wide segments as described for Seminole Design 7, *opposite*. The segments from the top and bottom strip sets are mirror images of each other.

Turning every other piece to alternate colors, sew the segments together as shown in Drawing B, *right*. Press seams to one side.

Patchwork band should measure approximately 44 inches.

TO ADD EDGING STRIPS: Cut two ⅞-inch-wide strips from the pink print fabric.

From the dark green fabric, cut two 2-inch-wide strips. Press the green strips in half, wrong sides facing, so they are 1 inch wide.

Matching raw edges, stitch a green strip to a pink strip. Repeat for the second pair of strips. Press the seam allowances toward the green strips.

Referring to Drawing C, *right*, sew pink portion of the edging strip sets to patchwork, ½ inch from the outer points of the zigzags. The dashed lines on the diagram indicate the approximate placement for the edging strips.

Press seams toward the edging strips. Trim excess patchwork, leaving ¼-inch seam allowances.

To trim the towels

Cut a piece of patchwork ½ inch longer than the width of the bath towel. Turn under ¼ inch on each end of the band.

Pin the wrong side of the band to the right side of the towel. Posi-

tion the band so it will cover any woven edge trim on the towel.

Topstitch band to towel.

Repeat to trim the hand towel.

To trim the washcloths

Cut one 1½-inch-wide strip *each* from the pink print fabric and the dark green fabric.

Press each strip in half lengthwise, wrong sides facing, so strips are ¾ inch wide. Matching raw edges, sew strips together. Press seams toward the green strip.

Plan trim placement on washcloth. Cut a piece of band ½ inch longer than the length of placement line.

Pin the band to the washcloth, turning the ends of the band under ¼ inch. Topstitch the band to the washcloth.

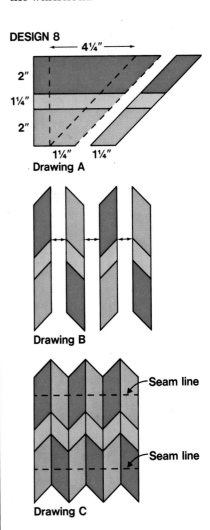

DESIGN 8

Drawing A

Drawing B

Drawing C

Seam line

Seam line

GARDEN PATH

YO-YO
COVERLET

◆ ◆ ◆

Create gorgeous patchwork lace by
stitching together an assortment
of "yo-yos," each made from a
gathered fabric circle. In this Garden
Path Yo-Yo Coverlet, double rows
of yo-yo paths form borders for flower
beds of multicolored print yo-yos.

1 Using a compass, draw a 4¼-inch-diameter circle on paper. Make a cardboard or plastic template for the circle. If you are using a cardboard template, make new templates when the old ones become worn.

To mark the fabric with the template, draw around template on the *wrong* side of the fabric; then cut out the circle. To speed the cutting, you may wish to cut circles from several layers of fabric at once.

2 To make a yo-yo, thread a needle and tie a knot in the end of the thread. Use strong thread, such as quilting thread or carpet thread, or use two strands of regular sewing thread.

With the wrong side facing up, hand-sew small running stitches around the circle, folding under ¼ inch to the *wrong side* as you sew. Begin stitching so the knot is positioned atop the narrow fold on the wrong side of the circle.

3 Pull on the thread to draw the outside of the circle to the center with the *wrong* side of the fabric hidden on the inside of the yo-yo. Pull thread up tightly to leave a small center opening; knot the thread.

Flatten the yo-yo slightly.

The gathered side of the yo-yo is the front or right side; the smooth side is the back.

4 To join yo-yos, place two yo-yos together with the fronts (gathered sides) facing. Using matching thread, whipstitch the circles together along one side.

Create blocks by sewing the yo-yos into rows; join the rows.

Yo-Yo Coverlet

Shown on pages 22 and 23.

Finished coverlet is approximately 72x88 inches.

MATERIALS
13½ yards of medium green fabric
Approximately 12 yards of assorted print fabric scraps
Cardboard or plastic for templates
Compass; paper

INSTRUCTIONS
Referring to the instructions, *left*, make a template for a 4¼-inch-diameter circle. The circle dimension includes ¼-inch seam allowances; *do not* add seam allowances when cutting the pieces from fabric.

TO MAKE ONE YO-YO BLOCK: Cut 24 circles from the green fabric; cut 25 circles from assorted print fabrics.

Referring to Step 2 and Step 3, make each circle into a yo-yo.

Referring to Step 4, piece a block in seven rows with seven yo-yos in each row.

To make the first and seventh rows, join seven green yo-yos. For each of the other rows, join five print yo-yos and two green yo-yos, placing a green yo-yo at the beginning and end of a row. Join the rows to complete the block.

Make 30 yo-yo blocks.

You will need 720 green yo-yos and 750 print yo-yos to complete the 30 blocks.

TO MAKE BORDERS: Cut 158 circles from green fabric. Make the circles into yo-yos.

For each side border, stitch together 42 yo-yos.

For the top and bottom borders, join 37 yo-yos for each border.

Sew borders to coverlet sides. Sew borders to the top and bottom of the coverlet.

Choosing Fabrics for Scrap Quilts

Although you can choose scrap fabrics haphazardly and add them to the quilt in random order, the most successful and most attractive scrap quilts are usually carefully planned.

As a general rule, the fabrics in a quilt should be of a similar weight and type. Choose firmly woven colorfast fabrics that do not ravel easily. Avoid limp or stretchy fabrics because they easily lose their shape. Heavy fabrics such as velvet, corduroy, and denim are difficult to hand-stitch.

Slick fabrics such as silk, satin, and taffeta may slip out of place as you stitch.

The fabrics should require similar care. If the quilt is to be laundered, choose fabrics that are washable. Prewash, dry, and iron the fabrics to remove the sizing; preshrink them, and check for colorfastness. If you use a variety of small irregularly shaped fabric pieces that may not have been

prewashed, hand-wash and dry them to avoid having them tangle and fray.

Traditional choices for quilts are 100 percent cotton and cotton-polyester blend fabrics. Many of the new cotton fabrics are treated with a permanent-press finish to make laundering easier. Calico, cotton broadcloth, and lightweight chintz—printed in dots, small prints, checks, and florals—are ideal fabrics for use in quilts.

BIAS
APPLIQUÉ

♦ ♦ ♦

Versatile bias fabric strips that easily flow around curves are a special way to decorate clothing or create such accessories as pillows, place mats, and wall hangings for your home. Here and on the following pages are a variety of intriguing designs and a tulip motif that simulates the art of stained glass. In the latter, fabrics replace the stained glass, and gray or black bias strips create the "leading."

The red plaid and muslin place mats and coordinating napkins at *left* provide a country setting for fresh pastries and a morning cup of coffee or cocoa.

The familiar heart motif, modified by adding a loop to the top, is a simple design on which to practice your bias appliqué skills. Bias strips will bend easily to flow around the gentle curves at the top of the heart, and the broad point at the heart tip allows ample space to tuck under the strips when mitering the corner.

Make heart pockets to hold coordinating napkins, as described in the project instructions on page 36, or work up a quicker version of the place mats by appliquéing the heart design directly onto purchased prequilted place mats.

1 Trace the apron pocket tulip pattern on page 37 onto tracing paper. Make paper patterns for the tulip petal and tulip tip underlays.

Cut a left and right tulip petal from red fabric. Cut a tulip tip from yellow fabric.

Using dressmaker's carbon paper and tracing paper, transfer the tulip design onto a 9-inch fabric square, positioning the design diagonally on the square.

Pin or baste the tulip petal and tip underlays within the corresponding design outlines, *above*.

3 Slip a ¼-inch-wide bias pressing bar into the sewn piece. Adjust the seam so it is centered on the back side. Press the strip flat. Continue to press the length of the strip, *above*, sliding the bias pressing bar along the inside of the strip.

Trim seams to ⅛ inch wide.

2 Fold a square of gray fabric in half diagonally. Using a rotary cutter and ruler, *above*, cut the fabric, parallel to the fold, into 1-inch-wide bias strips. When they are stitched and pressed, the strips will finish ¼ inch wide.

With wrong sides facing, press the strips in half lengthwise. Machine-stitch exactly ¼ inch from the fold to make ¼-inch-wide bias strips. To make other widths of bias strips, adjust the distance you stitch from the fold.

4 Pin or baste the prepared bias within the pattern guidelines.

Using thread to match the bias, appliqué the bias to the background fabric, *above*, stitching the underlays in place at the same time.

Stitching Celtic Designs

Because Celtic designs are continuous and don't have a beginning or an end, it may appear difficult to know where to begin when stitching the designs.

Begin basting a bias strip so the strip end will be in an under position, leaving a 1-inch tail to trim later. Working on a flat surface to help eliminate puckering, baste the strip along the design line, smoothing the strip as you work. End the strip and start a new strip in an under position, leaving 1-inch tails at the ending and beginning of the strips.

When you have basted a quadrant of the design, you can begin to appliqué the bias strips, using thread that matches the color of the strips.

One of the challenges of appliquéing Celtic designs is to bend the bias strips smoothly around the many curves. Begin by appliquéing the side of the bias along the *inside* edge of the curves; then stitch the side of the bias along the outside edge. If necessary, on particularly tight curves, lightly steam-press the outside edge of the strip before stitching to help it conform to the curve.

As you come to a place that covers beginning and ending tails, check to make sure the design is following the over-and-under pattern correctly. To finish the tails, pull them out from under the over-strip; trim the tails so they butt at the center of the over-strip. Return the tails to the under position, checking to be sure they are covered. Stitch the over-strip in place, securing the tails.

Yellow and red tulips decorate the bib and pocket of this blue chambray butcher apron, *above*. A row of tulips along the bottom of the apron forms a large pocket that is divided into three sections.

For the framed tulip picture and the tulip soft box, *opposite*, we used hand-dyed fabrics in shades of blue, peach, and green to resemble colored glass. The mottled, somewhat uneven, coloring of the hand-dyed fabrics creates the

illusion of the bubbles and swirls of color found in art glass. For the fabric "leading," appliqué ¼-inch-wide strips of dark gray or black bias over the raw edges of the fabric "glass" pieces.

BIAS APPLIQUÉ

The intricate interwoven bias appliqué designs for the wall hanging, *opposite*, and the pillows, *above*, were inspired by ancient Celtic designs. Two basic principles are followed in all Celtic designs. The designs are continuous—there is no beginning or ending—and only two lines intersect at any point.

Underlays, colorful pieces of fabric tucked under the bias strips, create centers of interest in the designs.

Ten shades of peach and rust fabrics, easily pieced on a sewing machine, form the underlay for the wall hanging.

Instructions for the wall hanging begin on page 40; instructions for the pillows begin on page 41.

Transform denim wardrobe basics into wearable art with bias appliqué. The simple, straight lines of the skirt *above* and jacket *opposite* are softened by the continuously curving and flowing bias strips.

Complete your outfit by sewing a coordinating purse. Stitch the purse from bright red polished cotton, and decorate the flap with the companion blue and white striped fabric.

When the bias strips are cut from striped fabric, such as for the projects shown on these two pages, the stripes appear to spiral around like the red and white stripes on a candy cane.

Project instructions for the items shown begin on page 44.

Heart Place Mats And Napkins

Shown on pages 26 and 27.

Finished place mats are approximately 12x18 inches.

MATERIALS
For two place mats and napkins
1½ yards of muslin
1½ yards of red plaid fabric
½ yard of polyester fleece
⅜-inch-wide bias pressing bar
Dressmaker's carbon paper and tracing wheel

INSTRUCTIONS
TO MAKE PLACE MATS: From the muslin, cut four 12x18-inch rectangles for the place mat tops and linings. Using a plate or similar round object as a guide, round the corners on two of the rectangles to form ovals.

From the fleece, cut two 12x18-inch rectangles.

From the red plaid fabric, cut six 3-inch-wide strips across the width of the red plaid fabric.

To make one place mat, sew the short ends of the three strips together into a loop. Press the ruffle in half, *wrong* sides facing, so it is 1½ inches wide. Run a gathering thread around the ruffle; gather. Baste the ruffle to the right side of each muslin oval.

Place a muslin rectangle atop a fleece rectangle. Center and pin a muslin oval atop layered pieces, *right* sides facing. Sew around oval, leaving an opening for turning. Trim excess fleece and muslin. Clip, turn, and stitch opening closed. Repeat to make a second place mat.

TO MAKE HEART POCKETS: Trace the heart design, *above right,* onto tracing paper. Referring to the small drawing of the complete design, expand the half design into the complete design.

From the red plaid fabric, cut a 24-inch square. Referring to the bias appliqué instructions on page 28, cut and prepare two ⅜-inch-wide strips that are each approximately 28 inches long.

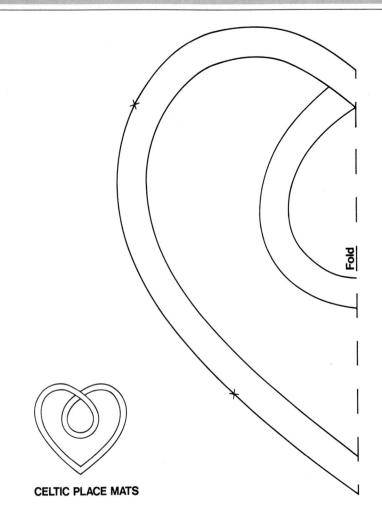

CELTIC PLACE MATS

To make one pocket, use dressmaker's carbon paper and a tracing wheel to transfer only the outline of the heart design onto a separate piece of muslin.

Allowing at least ½ inch for seam allowances, transfer a second heart onto another piece of muslin. Transfer the complete design to use as placement guidelines for the appliqué. Baste the bias strips along the placement lines on the heart, mitering the bias at the bottom of the heart. Appliqué the strips.

Cut out the hearts, adding ¼-inch seam allowances. Pin the hearts with right sides facing; sew around the outline, leaving an opening for turning. Clip, turn, and sew opening closed.

Pin the pocket to the left side of a place-mat top. Machine-top-stitch the pocket between the X marks along both sides of the heart. Repeat to make a pocket for the other place mat.

TO MAKE NAPKINS: Cut two 18-inch squares from the red plaid fabric. Serge or narrowly hem the edges.

Tulip Apron

Shown on pages 29 and 30.

Finished apron is approximately 29½ inches long.

MATERIALS
1 yard *each* of blue chambray and red and white striped fabrics
Scraps of red, yellow, and green fabrics
27-inch square of gray fabric
¼-inch-wide bias pressing bar
Tracing paper
Dressmaker's carbon paper and tracing wheel

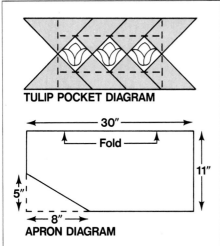

TULIP POCKET DIAGRAM

APRON DIAGRAM

30″ — Fold — 11″ — 5″ — 8″

INSTRUCTIONS

To make the pattern for the apron bib design, draw a 6¾-inch square on tracing paper. Trace the tulip pattern on page 39 within the square, tracing only one tulip and the right leaf. Do *not* trace the left leaf. To draw the left leaf, fold the paper in half diagonally and trace the right leaf onto the left side of the stem to be a mirror image of the right one.

Trace the pattern for the tulip pocket design, *below right.*

TO CUT PIECES: From the blue chambray fabric, cut a 22x30-inch rectangle for the apron. Fold the rectangle in half, lengthwise. Referring to the Apron Diagram, *above,* cut away the triangle indicated by the dashed lines to create the apron armholes.

From the remaining chambray, cut a 7½x22-inch piece for the pocket lining. For the patchwork pieces for the pocket, cut four 6½-inch squares. Cut each square in half diagonally into two triangles. Triangles include ¼-inch seam allowances. (You will have a total of eight triangles.)

From red and white striped fabric, cut a 9-inch square for the apron bib, positioning the square so that the stripes run diagonally through the square. For the tulip pocket, cut three 5½-inch squares with the stripes running diagonally through the squares.

From remaining striped fabric, cut approximately 5½ yards of 1½-inch-wide bias. Press ¼ inch to the *wrong* side along the raw edges of the bias. Press bias in half, *wrong* sides facing.

Referring to the bias appliqué instructions on page 28, cut the gray fabric square into 1-inch-wide strips. Using the bias pressing bar, prepare ¼-inch-wide bias strips.

Adding ⅛-inch seam allowances, cut the underlay pieces. From the red fabric, cut one A tulip tip, three B tulip petals, and three reverse B tulip petals.

From yellow fabric, cut three A tulip tips, one B tulip petal, and one reverse B tulip petal.

From green fabric, cut one C leaf and one reverse C leaf.

TO MAKE BIB DESIGN: Using dressmaker's carbon paper and a tracing wheel, transfer the tulip design to the 9-inch square, centering the design.

Pin or baste a yellow tulip tip and red tulip petals within the corresponding design outlines.

Pin or baste the gray bias strips along the design lines in the order shown on the pattern, adding the pieces for the left leaf. Appliqué the bias strips.

Baste bias strips around the perimeter of the square, outlining the design and covering the ends of the other strips. Trim any excess red and white striped fabric that extends beyond the bias.

Pin the bib design to the apron center, 2 inches from the top. Appliqué the strips around the perimeter of the square, attaching the bib to the apron.

TO MAKE POCKET: Transfer the tulip pocket design onto each 5½-inch stripe square. Refer to the bias appliqué instructions on page 28 to appliqué the tulips to the squares. Make one yellow tulip with a red tip and two red tulips with yellow tips.

Referring to the Tulip Pocket Diagram, *top left,* sew squares to chambray triangles. The triangles are oversized; trim excess triangles to form a rectangle, leaving ¼-inch seams. With right sides facing, sew top edge of the pocket to the pocket lining.

Draw a placement line along the apron 5 inches from the bottom edge. With right sides facing, pin the lower pocket edge along the placement line. Stitch pocket to apron. Turn pocket up, press. Baste pocket sides to the apron. Machine-stitch between tulips to form three pocket sections.

continued

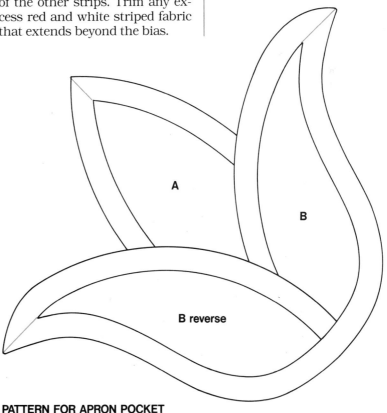

A

B

B reverse

PATTERN FOR APRON POCKET

FINISHING: Encase the apron top edge with bias. Encase the straight side edges and the bottom edge as one unit, mitering the corners. For the neck and ties, cut a 2¾-yard-long piece of bias. Mark a point 10 inches to each side of center of bias strip. Match each marked point to one side of the apron top edge, forming the neck loop. Machine-topstitch bias edges, forming ties, a neck loop, and encasing the armholes.

Tulip Soft Box

Shown on page 31.

The box is 7¾ inches square.

MATERIALS
¾ yard of light blue fabric
18-inch square of gray fabric
Peach, orange, and green fabric scraps
¾ yard of polyester fleece
¼-inch-wide bias pressing bar
Two 7¾-inch-square pieces of cardboard or mat board
Four 2¾x7¾-inch pieces of cardboard or mat board
Tracing paper; graph paper
Dressmaker's carbon paper and tracing wheel

INSTRUCTIONS
Draw the tulip pattern as directed in the instructions on page 37 for the bib of the Tulip Apron.

Referring to the diagram, *right,* draw the box pattern onto graph paper. Draw tulip pattern onto box pattern in the position indicated on diagram.

TO APPLIQUÉ DESIGN: From the blue fabric, cut two 20x24-inch pieces. Using dressmaker's carbon paper and a tracing wheel, transfer the box pattern and the tulip design onto one blue piece.

Adding ⅛-inch seam allowances, cut underlays from fabric scraps. Cut one A tulip tip from orange fabric. Cut one B tulip petal and one reverse B petal from peach fabric. Cut one C leaf and one reverse C leaf from green fabric. Baste underlays within corresponding outlines.

Referring to bias appliqué instructions on page 28, cut the gray fabric square into 1-inch-wide strips. Prepare ¼-inch-wide bias strips.

Following the instructions on page 37 for the Tulip Apron bib design, appliqué the tulip design.

TO MAKE BOX: Baste fleece atop the wrong side of box fabric, stitching along the box outline. With *right* sides facing, pin box fabric atop matching lining piece; sew around box outline. Trim excess batting and fabric; clip. Slit blue lining fabric *only* along line AB. Turn right side out through the opening.

To insert the cardboard, slip one 7¾-inch square through the slit into tulip portion of box. Using a zipper foot, machine-stitch along the edge of the cardboard.

Insert the smaller cardboard pieces into the box. Stitch along the pieces. Insert the remaining cardboard square into the box bottom. Stitch the slit closed. Fold up box sides; stitch sides together to form the box.

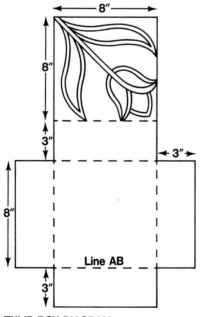

TULIP BOX DIAGRAM

Framed Tulips

Shown on page 31.

The tulip design is approximately 12¼ inches square, excluding the frame.

MATERIALS
18-inch square *each* of light blue fabric, muslin, and polyester fleece
Scraps of peach, orange, royal blue, and green fabrics
36-inch square of gray fabric
¼-inch-wide bias pressing bar
Dressmaker's carbon paper
Tracing wheel; tracing paper
Purchased picture frame

INSTRUCTIONS
Fold a 13-inch square of tracing paper in half lengthwise and crosswise, creating four square divisions. Trace the tulip design, *opposite,* onto the top left quadrant. Rotating the design around the center, complete the design.

Using dressmaker's carbon paper and a tracing wheel, transfer the tulip design to the blue fabric square, centering the design.

Adding ⅛-inch seam allowances, cut the underlays. Cut two A tulip tips from peach fabric. Cut two B tulip petals and two reverse B tulip petals *each* from the royal blue and orange fabrics. Cut four C leaves and four reverse C leaves from green fabric. The light blue background fabric will form the tulip tips on the blue tulips.

Referring to the photograph on page 31 for color placement, baste the underlays within the corresponding outlines.

Referring to the bias appliqué instructions on page 28, cut the gray fabric square into 1-inch-wide strips and prepare ¼-inch-wide bias strips.

Pin or baste bias along design lines in the approximate order shown on pattern, reserving longest bias pieces for the longest "leading lines." Baste bias strips around the perimeter, covering strip ends; appliqué.

Layer muslin, fleece, and design. Baste around the perimeter. Frame as desired.

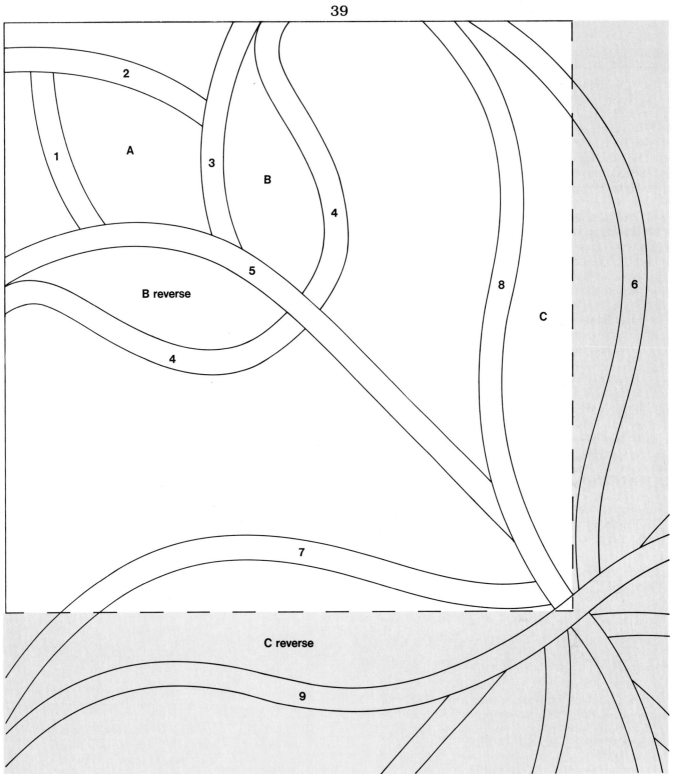

TULIP DESIGN FOR APRON, SOFT BOX, AND FRAMED TULIPS

FRAMED TULIP DIAGRAM

Celtic Wall Hanging

Shown on page 32.

The finished wall hanging is approximately 42 inches square, excluding framing.

MATERIALS
¼ yard *each* of 10 shades of fabric, ranging from light peach to deep rust
1¼ yards *each* of royal blue, teal, and light green fabrics
1¼ yards of white-on-white printed muslin
42-inch square *each* of muslin and polyester batting or fleece
Bias pressing bars in the following widths: 3/16 inch, 3/8 inch, and ½ inch
Large sheets of paper for patterns
Dressmaker's carbon paper
Tracing wheel

INSTRUCTIONS
Note: Measurements include ¼-inch seam allowances.

Enlarge the Celtic pattern, *right,* onto paper. Make a pattern for the underlay, which is the shaded area on the pattern.

FOR BACKGROUND: Arrange the peach and light fabrics in order from the lightest fabric to the darkest. Number the fabrics from 1 to 10, numbering the darkest Fabric 10.

From Fabric 10, the darkest rust fabric, cut four 5-inch squares. From remaining peach and rust fabrics, cut 1¼-inch-wide strips across the width of the fabric. Set the Fabric 1 strips, the lightest peach, aside.

To make the pieced underlay, begin by piecing one quadrant of the design. Referring to Figure 1, *opposite,* sew a Fabric 9 strip to one side of the rust square; trim strip even with the square. Press the seam allowances away from the square.

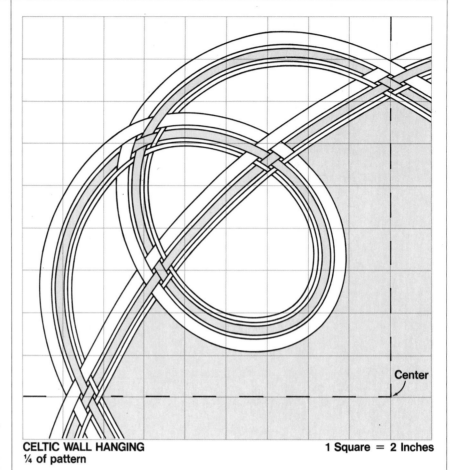

CELTIC WALL HANGING
¼ of pattern

1 Square = 2 Inches

Center

Sew a Fabric 9 strip to the adjacent side and across the end of the first strip; trim strip even with the square. Press seam allowances away from the square.

Continue to add strips of Fabric 8 to Fabric 2 in the order listed in Figure 1 to the same two sides of the square. Do *not* add the Fabric 1 strips at this time.

Repeat to make a total of four pieced quadrants.

Referring to Figure 2, *opposite,* join two quadrants with a Fabric 1 (lightest peach) strip between them, positioning the quadrants as shown. Trim the Fabric 1 strip even with the quadrants. Repeat to join two more quadrants.

Join the pairs of quadrants, placing a Fabric 1 strip between them. Trim the Fabric 1 strip even with the quadrants.

Using the underlay pattern, cut an underlay from the pieced fabric, adding approximately ⅛-inch seam allowances.

From the printed muslin, cut a 42-inch square for the background of the design. Fold the square in fourths to determine the center. Lightly press along the fold lines.

Using the dressmaker's carbon paper and a tracing wheel, transfer the Celtic design to the printed muslin. Baste the underlay to the muslin background.

TO MAKE CELTIC DESIGN: To make the bias strips, cut one 42-inch square *each* from the blue, the teal, and the green fabrics.

Referring to the bias appliqué instructions on page 28, cut the light green square into ¾-inch-wide bias strips. Using the 3/16-inch-wide bias pressing bar, prepare the bias strips.

Cut 1¼-inch-wide bias strips from the teal fabric square. Using the 3/8-inch-wide bias pressing bar, prepare the strips.

Cut 1½-inch-wide bias strips from the blue fabric square. Using the ½-inch-wide bias pressing bar, prepare the strips.

Pin or baste the blue bias within the design lines that were transferred to the background fabric, making sure the bias covers the raw edges of the underlay.

Following established weaving pattern, baste teal strips ⅛ inch to the inside of the blue strips.

In a similar manner and following the established weaving pattern, baste the green strips ⅛ inch inside the teal strips.

Appliqué the strips to the background, using thread to match the strips.

TO FINISH: Layer wall hanging, fleece or batting, and muslin backing. Mount the hanging on wooden stretcher bars or have it professionally framed.

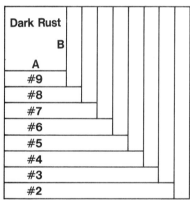

Figure 1

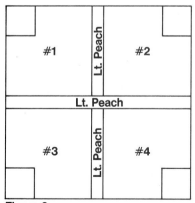

Figure 2

Celtic Pillows

Shown on page 33.

The finished corded pillow is 19 inches square; the blue plaid pillow is 22 inches square.

MATERIALS
¾ yard of navy fabric
⅝ yard of white-on-white printed muslin
¼-inch-wide bias pressing bar
Tracing paper
Dressmaker's carbon paper and tracing wheel

For the corded pillow
½ yard of brick red fabric
24-inch square of blue, rust, and navy striped fabric
2½ yards of ¼-inch-diameter cotton cable cord
Polyester fiberfill

For the blue plaid pillow
⅝ yard of blue plaid fabric
¼ yard of polyester fleece or batting
Scrap of navy fabric
18-inch square pillow form

INSTRUCTIONS
Trace the Celtic patterns on pages 42 and 43. Referring to the small drawings on the pattern pages, expand the quarter-patterns into the full designs. The shaded areas on the patterns are the patterns for the underlays; make patterns for the underlays.

To make the corded pillow
From the muslin fabric, cut one 19-inch square for the pillow front. Using dressmaker's carbon paper and a tracing wheel, transfer the pillow design on page 43 to the pillow front.

From the brick red fabric, cut two of underlay piece A and two of underlay piece B, adding ⅛-inch seam allowances.

From the navy fabric, cut a 19-inch square for the pillow back. Cut two of underlay piece A and two of underlay piece C, adding ⅛-inch seam allowances.

Referring to the photograph on page 33, baste the underlays to the pillow front within the corresponding outlines.

Referring to the bias appliqué instructions on page 28, cut the striped fabric square into 1-inch-wide strips. Using the ¼-inch-wide bias pressing bar, prepare the strips.

Pin or baste the bias strips along the design lines, making sure the bias covers the raw edges of the underlays.

Using thread to match the bias strips, appliqué the strips to the pillow front.

From the remaining brick red fabric, cut bias strips to cover the cording. Using a zipper foot, baste the bias over the cording.

Baste the covered cording to the pillow front along the seam line.

With right sides facing, sew the pillow front to the pillow back, leaving an opening for turning. Clip, turn, and stuff. Stitch the opening closed.

To make the blue plaid pillow
From the muslin, cut a 16½-inch square for the pillow front.

Using dressmaker's carbon paper and a tracing wheel, transfer the design on page 42 to the pillow front.

From the navy fabric, cut one 7¼x16½-inch rectangle and one 13¾x16½-inch rectangle for the pillow back. From the remaining navy fabric, cut the underlay, adding ⅛-inch seam allowances.

Baste the underlay to the pillow front within the outline.

From blue plaid fabric, cut an 18-inch square for the bias strips. Cut four 4½x24½-inch rectangles and four 4½x16½-inch rectangles for the pillow trim.

From the polyester fleece, cut two 4½x24½-inch rectangles and two 4½x16½-inch rectangles for the trim lining. Cut a 16½-inch square for the pillow front lining.
continued

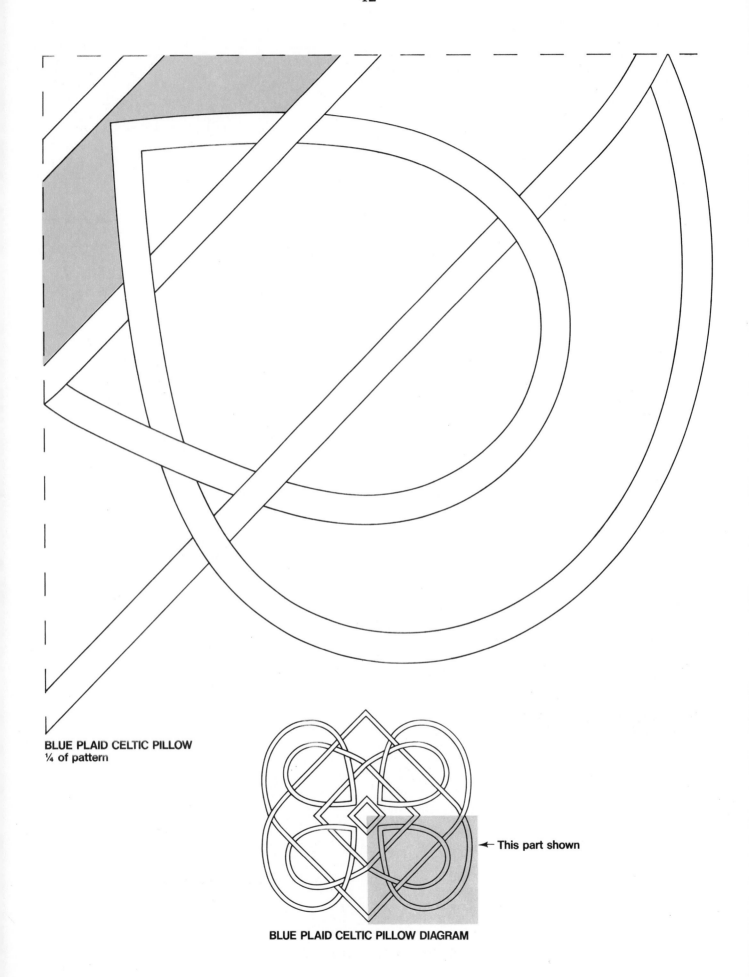

BLUE PLAID CELTIC PILLOW
¼ of pattern

← This part shown

BLUE PLAID CELTIC PILLOW DIAGRAM

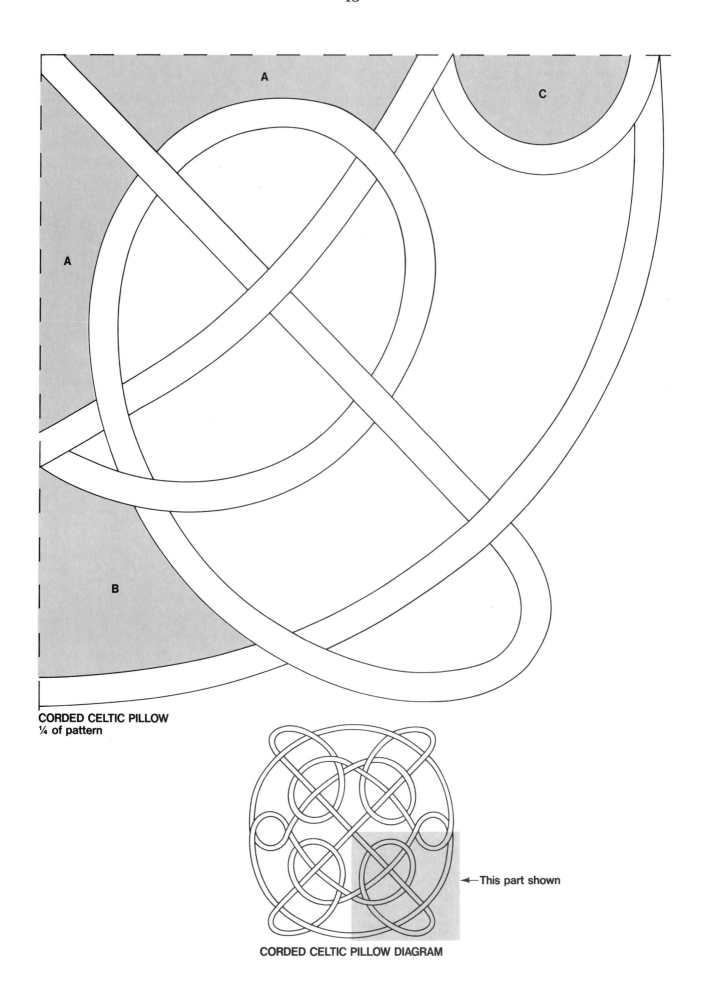

CORDED CELTIC PILLOW
¼ of pattern

A
C
A
B

This part shown

CORDED CELTIC PILLOW DIAGRAM

Baste the fleece square to the *wrong* side of the pillow front. Baste fleece pieces to the *wrong* side of matching trim pieces. Half of the trim pieces are unlined.

Referring to the bias appliqué instructions on page 28, cut the 18-inch blue plaid square into 1-inch-wide bias strips. Using the bias pressing bar, prepare ¼-inch-wide bias strips.

Pin or baste the bias strips along the design lines, making sure the bias covers the raw edges of the fabric underlays.

Using matching thread, appliqué the strips to the pillow front.

To make the envelope back, press 1¼ inches to the *wrong* side of one 16½-inch side of each pillow back piece; hem. Overlap the hemmed edge of the larger piece over the hemmed edge of the smaller piece, forming a 16½-inch square; baste.

Sew the 16½-inch-long fleece-lined trim pieces to opposite sides of the pillow front. Sew the longer fleece-lined trim pieces to the remaining two sides.

Repeat to add the unlined trim pieces to the pillow back.

With *right* sides facing, sew the pillow front to the pillow back. Clip seams. Turn pillow through envelope opening. Press the edges with a cool iron, taking care not to melt the fleece.

Align the pillow front with the pillow back; stitch around the pillow front outline along the trim seams through all layers. Insert the pillow form.

Jacket and Skirt

Shown on pages 34 and 35.

MATERIALS
Purchased denim jacket and skirt
36-inch square of red and white striped fabric
Tissue paper
Tracing paper
Dressmaker's carbon paper and tracing wheel
3/16-inch-wide bias pressing bar

INSTRUCTIONS
Referring to the bias appliqué instructions on page 28, cut the red and white striped fabric square into 1-inch-wide strips. Using the bias pressing bar, prepare 3/16-inch-wide bias strips.

To make the skirt
Trace the Celtic pattern for the skirt, *below,* onto tracing paper.

Measure circumference of your skirt approximately 2 to 3 inches above the skirt hem. Make a master pattern of the skirt by cutting a piece of tissue paper this length, taping together pieces if necessary. Mark the positions of the side seams, center front, and center back on the tissue paper.

Beginning at the center front, trace the Celtic skirt design onto the tissue paper master pattern, repeating the design along the length of the master pattern.

Using dressmaker's carbon paper and a tracing wheel, transfer the design to the skirt.

Baste bias strips along the design lines. Appliqué the strips.

To make the jacket
Note: Because jacket sizes and styles vary, no pattern for the jacket is given.

Trace the yoke portion of the jacket back and jacket fronts onto large sheets of tissue paper. Tape the sheets together at the shoulders to form the complete yoke portion of the jacket.

Referring to the photograph on page 35, plan your own Celtic design on the tissue paper pattern. Fold the tissue paper in half along the center back; draw the design on one half. Trace the design onto the other half. Plan the placement of the design so it is not covered by the jacket collar. Using dressmaker's carbon paper and a tracing wheel, transfer design to jacket yoke.

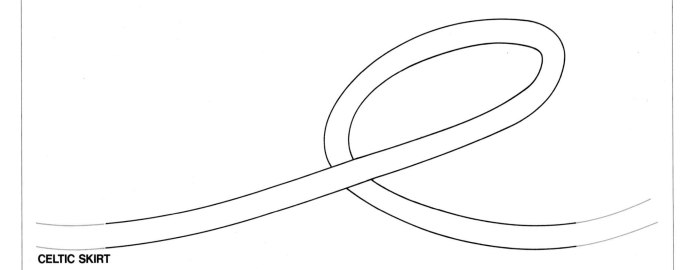

CELTIC SKIRT

CELTIC PURSE

Pin or baste the prepared bias strips along the design lines. Using matching thread, appliqué the strips to the jacket.

Celtic Purse

Shown on page 34.

The finished purse is approximately 6x8½ inches.

MATERIALS
⅝ yard of red fabric
1 yard of blue and white striped fabric
⅝ yard of polyester fleece
¼-inch-wide bias pressing bar
Large sheets of paper for patterns; tracing paper
Dressmaker's carbon paper and tracing wheel

INSTRUCTIONS
Trace the pattern, *above*, onto tracing paper.

To make the purse pattern, draw a 9x19-inch rectangle on paper. Round the corners on one end only. To make the purse side pattern, draw a 2⅛x5⅛-inch rectangle. Round the corners on one narrow end only. The patterns include ¼-inch seam allowances.

Using the purse pattern, cut one *each* from the red fabric, the striped fabric, and the fleece.

Using the purse side pattern, cut two *each* from the red fabric and the striped fabric.

For the purse strap, cut two pieces, each 2x20 inches, from the red fabric.

Using dressmaker's carbon paper and a tracing wheel, transfer the design to the rounded end of the red purse piece.

Cut a 24-inch square from the striped fabric. Referring to the bias appliqué instructions on page 28, cut the square into 1-inch-wide bias strips. Using the ¼-inch-wide bias pressing bar, prepare bias strips.

Pin or baste the bias strips along the design lines. Using thread to match the bias, appliqué the strips.

Baste the fleece to the wrong side of the purse.

To attach one purse side, pin one long edge of the purse side to the long edge of the undecorated end of the purse. Ease the purse piece around the rounded corner of the end piece; continue pinning along the next long side. Stitch the purse side to the purse. Repeat to add the other side piece.

In a similar manner, assemble the purse lining from the lining side pieces and purse lining piece.

To make the strap, join strap pieces into one long piece. Press strap in half, lengthwise. Press long raw edges into center; topstitch. Attach strap ends to top of purse sides.

With right sides facing, sew the lining to the purse, leaving an opening for turning. Clip, turn, press, and stitch opening closed.

CATHEDRAL WINDOW

♦ ♦ ♦

Take-along sewing projects are always popular with stitchers. Because this Cathedral Window Coverlet, *below,* is made in sections, it's very portable and easy to work on away from home. Cut the insets all from one fabric, or cut them from a variety of fabric scraps.

Cathedral Window Coverlet

Shown on pages 46 and 47.

The finished coverlet is approximately 81x94 inches.

MATERIALS

30 yards of muslin
4 yards of light blue print fabric
Cardboard or plastic for
templates
Graph paper

INSTRUCTIONS

On graph paper, draw a 7¼-inch square and a 2-inch square. Pattern measurements include ¼-inch seam allowances. Make cardboard or plastic templates for the squares. If you use cardboard templates, replace the templates as the edges become worn.

From the blue print fabric, cut 1,396 squares, each 2 inches square, for the window inserts.

From the muslin, cut 725 squares, each 7¼ inches square, for the Cathedral Window units.

Referring to the instructions, *right,* follow Steps 1-5 to make 725 Cathedral Window units.

Construct the coverlet in five sections. Referring to Step 6 and Step 7, assemble 29 units into a row. Make five rows.

Join the rows to complete one coverlet section.

Referring to Step 7 and Step 8, add the inserts to the coverlet section. *Do not* add inserts to the partial windows around the outer perimeter. These inserts will be added after the sections have been joined.

Repeat the above instructions to make a total of five sections. Join the five sections.

Add inserts to the new windows that were created when the sections were joined. To finish the outer partial windows, roll the edges over the muslin and blindstitch in place.

Cathedral Window Assembly

Refer to the diagrams, *opposite,* to complete each step.

1 To make one Cathedral Window unit, cut one 7¼-inch square from muslin.

2 Fold the square in half. Taking ¼-inch seams, sew across the short ends.

3 Pull the unsewn edges apart at the center; flatten the unit into a square with the seamed edges meeting at the center.

Sew the remaining raw edges, leaving an opening approximately 1¼ inches long between the center and the corner for turning. Press the seams flat.

4 Turn the square right side out; press the square flat. If desired, blindstitch the opening closed. The square should measure approximately 4¾ inches.

5 With the seamed side of the square up, fold and tack each corner to the center, stitching through all layers. The square should now measure 3¼ inches.

Repeat Steps 1–5 to make the number of units needed.

6 With right sides facing, hand-stitch squares together into a row. Make the number of rows specified in the instructions.

7 In a similar manner, stitch the rows together to form a coverlet section. (The diagram for Step 7 shows only a small portion of a coverlet section.)

8 From printed fabric, cut the number of 2-inch-square inserts listed in the instructions.

Pin a fabric insert in a "window," where two units are joined. Insert positions are shaded in the diagram for Step 7.

Roll edges of muslin units over the inserts, tapering the folded edges at the corners. Blindstitch through all layers.

Add an insert in every window.

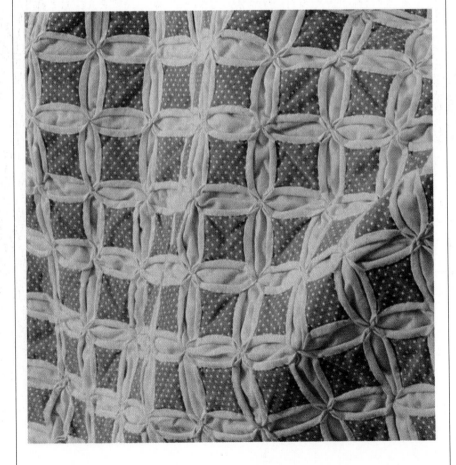

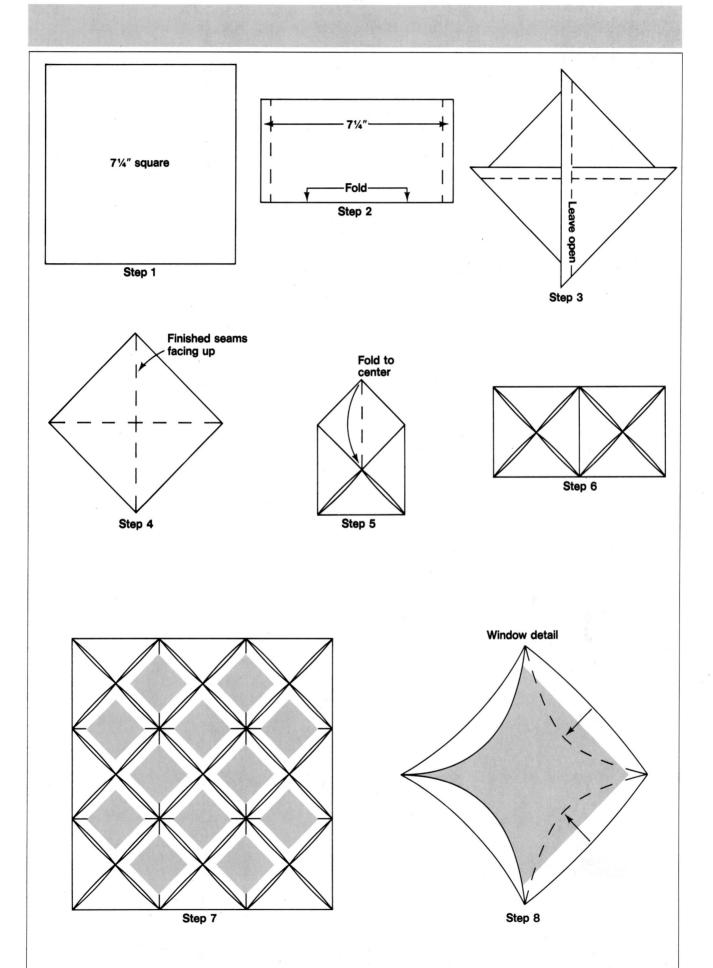

7¼" square

Step 1

7¼"

Fold

Step 2

Leave open

Step 3

Finished seams
facing up

Step 4

Fold to
center

Step 5

Step 6

Step 7

Window detail

Step 8

SHADOW APPLIQUÉ

FOR LITTLE FOLKS

Welcome a newborn with a lovingly stitched quilt worked in delicate shadow appliqué. Here and on the following four pages, you'll find a quilt and accompanying accessories sure to delight parents and child.

Shadow appliqué is a faster and simpler way than traditional appliqué to create a hand-stitched quilt and room accessories. Colorful fabric shapes are fused in place, eliminating the need to turn under the fabric edges. The background is then covered with a sheer overlay fabric that subdues the colors. Hand-quilting and embroidery hold layers in place and enhance the designs.

On the 31x45-inch quilt at *left,* whimsical girls and boys chase animals across 11-inch square blocks. On each of the six blocks are a child, an animal, and the letters spelling out the animal's name.

The inset on the back chair cushion *opposite* repeats one of the figures from the quilt. Accompanying flower and butterfly motifs decorate the curtain tiebacks *opposite.*

SHADOW APPLIQUÉ

1 Using a black permanent felt-tip pen, trace the patterns for the girl and the cat on page 58 onto tracing paper. Trace the cat so it is sitting in front of the girl.

Using a chalk pencil, trace the appliqué design on the background fabric square to create placement guidelines for the appliqué shapes. Use a letter stencil to draw the letters for the word "cat" vertically on the block.

Working from the *wrong* side of the traced pattern, trace the appliqué shapes onto the paper side of the fusible webbing. *Note:* When fused onto the appliqué fabrics, the shapes will be reversed.

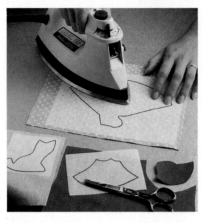

2 Cut out the pieces from the webbing, cutting the pieces in rough blocks larger than the drawn shapes.

Following the manufacturer's instructions, fuse the webbing to the *wrong* side of the appropriate fabric scraps. Cut out shapes; *do not* add seam allowances when cutting the pieces.

For the girl, cut two shoes from black fabric. Cut one arm from pink fabric. From assorted fabrics of your choice, cut the following pieces: one dress, one apron, one hat, the cat, and the letters for the word "cat."

Choosing Fabrics For Your Project

Choosing fabrics for shadow appliqué is different from choosing fabrics for a traditional appliqué project. The overlay fabric alters the appearance of fabrics used in the project.

Choose brightly colored fabrics for the appliqué pieces because the colors will appear more subdued when covered or "shadowed" by the sheer overlay fabric. For example, if you want an area to appear pink in the finished project, choose an intense pink or perhaps even a red fabric for the appliqué piece.

Printed fabrics and solid-color fabrics work equally well for shadow appliqué. The outlines of the printed designs are often somewhat blurred by the sheer overlay fabric, which softens the design. If you want the printed fabrics to retain a distinct printed appearance, choose fabrics with high color contrast and with bold, distinct design outlines.

Batiste, organdy, voile, and organza all are appropriate choices for the sheer overlay fabric, depending on the degree of shadowing you wish to achieve. Some sheer fabrics, such as organza, are quite transparent and will not greatly alter the appearance of the appliqué fabrics. On the other hand, more opaque overlay fabrics, such as batiste or voile, will noticeably alter and subdue the fabrics they cover.

To test the effect of the overlay fabric you intend to use, lay the appliqué fabrics on the background fabric. Cover the colored fabrics with the sheer overlay fabric to see how they will look when shadowed. You may want to adjust the color intensity of the appliqué fabrics and background fabric or use a more or a less opaque overlay fabric to achieve the results you desire.

3 Fuse each piece within the appropriate placement guideline on the background square, working from the background to the foreground.

Using a chalk pencil, draw any embroidery details such as the hat band, flower, and flower stem.

Using a black permanent fine-tip pen, draw detail lines, such as the cat's whiskers, that you do not want to embroider.

4 Cut a piece of sheer overlay fabric the size of the background block. Place the overlay atop the block; baste around the outer edges. If the edges of the sheer fabric tend to fray, coat them with commercial fray-preventer or clear nail polish.

Assemble the project according to the project instructions. After the project is assembled, quilt around the appliqué pieces.

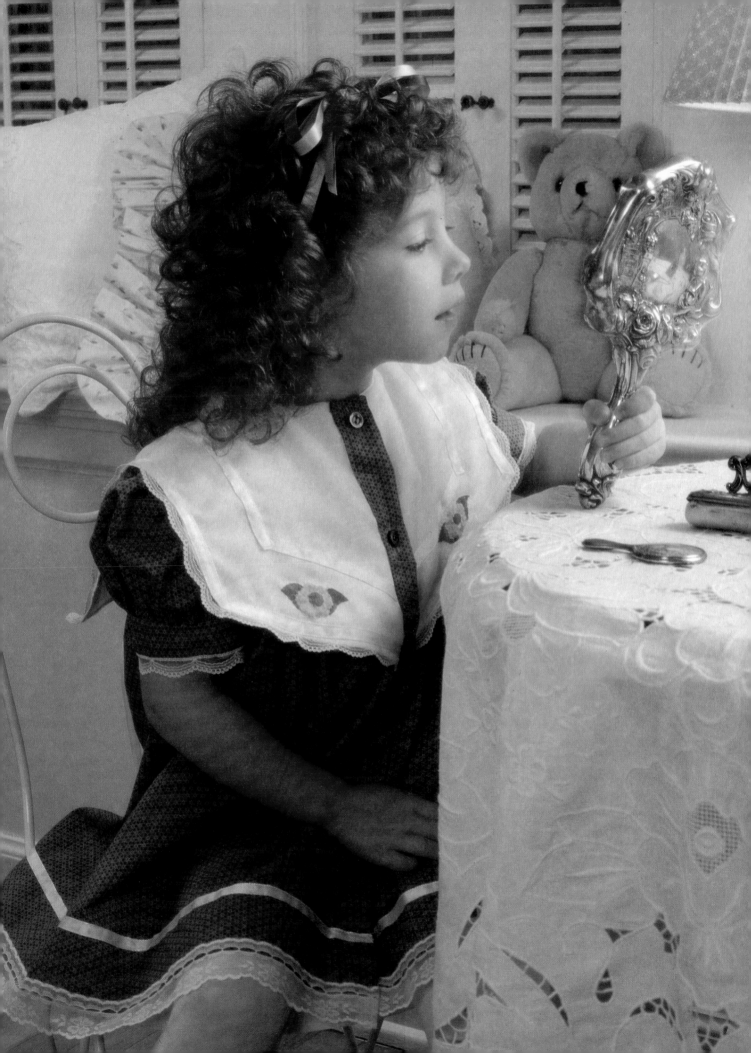

So Baby's older sister won't feel left out, sew her a special dress to wear to welcome her new brother or sister.

Using a commercial dress pattern, stitch the dress from a tiny print fabric. Trim the hem, sleeve bands, and collar with rows of ribbon and lace. Add a hand-stitched touch with delicate shadow appliqué flowers along the lower edge of the large, white collar in colors to coordinate with the dress fabric.

Older children might want to help choose the fabrics and motifs for a special baby's bib. Get out your scrap bag and let them pick out brightly colored fabrics for the appliqués. For the designs, choose the butterfly and tulip motifs *above,* let the youngsters draw their own designs, or use drawings with simple shapes, such as those found in children's coloring books.

Instructions for the projects in this chapter begin on page 56.

Shadow Appliqué Baby Quilt

Shown on pages 50–51 and 53.

The finished quilt is 31x45 inches; finished block is 11 inches square.

MATERIALS
¾ yard of white cotton fabric
¾ yard of white sheer fabric, such as polyester organza or voile
3 yards of lavender print fabric
Scraps of black fabric for the shoes
Scraps of pink fabric for the hands
Scraps of assorted brightly colored print and solid fabrics for appliqués
Paper-backed fusible webbing
Purchased alphabet stencil set for 1½-inch-high letters (available at variety or office supply stores)
Tailor's chalk pencils
Black fine-tip permanent marking pen
Crib-size quilt batting
Tracing paper
Assorted colors of embroidery floss to coordinate with the appliqué fabrics

INSTRUCTIONS
Measurements for quilt blocks and setting strips include ¼-inch seam allowances.

Trace the appliqué patterns on pages 58 and 59. The dashed lines on the patterns indicate outlines for pieces that are partially covered by other shapes. The blue lines indicate quilting and embroidery lines. Patterns are finished size; do not add seam allowances when cutting the fabric pieces.

TO CUT PIECES: For the quilt blocks, cut six 11½-inch squares from the white cotton fabric. For the overlays, cut matching pieces from the sheer fabric.

From lavender fabric, cut three 3½x39½-inch setting strips, two 3½x31½-inch setting strips, and four 3½x11½-inch setting strips. Set the remaining fabric aside.

TO MAKE GIRL BLOCKS: Refer to the instructions for Shadow Appliqué on page 52 to prepare and cut the appliqué pieces for the blocks.

Make three girl blocks. Make a girl with a cat and a girl with a hen facing right; make a girl with a lamb facing left.

Position the appliqué pieces for one girl, one animal, and the letters for the animal's name on each of the white blocks. Fuse pieces, working from background to foreground.

Using a permanent marking pen, draw details as follows: the wing, eye, and tail on the hen and the whiskers on the cat.

TO MAKE BOY BLOCKS: Use a chalk pencil to draw placement guidelines for the boy on three white background squares. Draw two boys facing left, the blocks with the pig and the duck; draw one boy facing right, the block with the dog. Draw placement guidelines for the animal and the letters for the animal's name on each block.

Draw shapes on fusible webbing. Fuse and cut pieces for three boy blocks.

For each boy, cut pieces as follows: two shoes from black fabric, one hand from pink fabric, and one shirt, overall, and hat from assorted fabric scraps.

Cut one pig, one duck, one dog, the letters for the animals' names, and two 1-inch-diameter circles for balloons from assorted fabric scraps.

Using a black pen, draw eyes and a tail on the pig. Draw eyes on the duck.

Position the appliqué shapes within the corresponding placement guidelines. Fuse the pieces to the block, working from the background to the foreground.

TO ADD DETAILS FOR EMBROIDERY: Using a chalk pencil, draw details on the blocks. Draw bands on the hats, simple flowers in the girls' hands, balloon strings on the balloons, a collar on the lamb, and a collar and leash on the dog. Draw feet and a beak on both the duck and the hen. Draw a fishing pole, a fishing line, and a fish on the block with the duck.

Using embroidery floss to coordinate with the clothing, outline-stitch the hat bands.

Using stitches and floss colors of your choice, embroider details on blocks.

ASSEMBLY: Cover the blocks with sheer fabric; baste around the perimeter.

Placing 3½x11½-inch sashing pieces between the blocks, sew the pig, lamb, and duck blocks into a vertical row. In a similar manner, sew the cat, dog, and hen blocks into a row.

Join the rows, placing a 3½x39½-inch setting strip at the beginning, at the end, and between the rows. Sew a 3½x31½-inch setting strip to the top and bottom of the quilt.

FINISHING: Cut the quilt back from the lavender print fabric. Cut the quilt back and batting 3 inches larger on all sides than the quilt top. Layer the quilt top, batting, and quilt back; baste.

Outline-quilt close to all appliqué shapes. Add additional quilting as desired.

From the remaining lavender fabric, cut approximately 5 yards of 2¼-inch-wide bias for the binding. With wrong sides facing, press the binding in half so it is 1⅛ inches wide. Sew the binding to the quilt.

Trim the excess batting and quilt back even with the quilt top. Blindstitch the folded edge of the binding to the quilt back.

Curtain Tiebacks

Shown on page 50.

The finished tiebacks are 4x24 inches.

MATERIALS
¼ yard *each* of lavender print fabric and white sheer fabric
½ yard of white broadcloth
Scraps of 2 lavender print fabrics and black, lavender, and green fabrics
¼ yard of polyester batting
Paper-backed fusible webbing
Two ¾-inch-diameter white plastic rings
Black embroidery floss
Tailor's chalk pencils
Tracing paper

INSTRUCTIONS
Trace the pansy and the butterfly patterns on page 61.

Cut two 4x24-inch rectangles *each* from the sheer fabric, the lavender print fabric, and the white broadcloth.

. Referring to Shadow Appliqué instructions on pages 52 and 53, prepare and cut the pieces for the appliqués. Cut two pieces *each* as follows: butterflies from the lightest lavender print fabric, butterfly bodies from the black fabric, pansies from the dark lavender print fabric, and pansy centers from the lavender fabric. Cut four leaves from the green fabric.

Mark placement guidelines on the white fabric rectangles. Trace a butterfly approximately 4½ inches from one end of each rectangle. Trace a pansy and leaves on each rectangle approximately 1 inch from the butterfly. The appliqué pieces should be centered on one-half of the rectangle.

To make one tieback, fuse a butterfly within placement guidelines; fuse a body atop butterfly.

Fuse the leaves within the corresponding guidelines. Fuse one pansy atop the leaves. Fuse a pansy center atop the flower.

Using a chalk pencil, draw the butterfly antennae. Using black embroidery floss, outline-stitch the antennae.

Place a sheer fabric rectangle atop the rectangle; baste around the perimeter.

Layer and baste the tieback, the batting, and the lavender print lining piece.

Outline-quilt close to the appliqué pieces; add additional quilting as desired.

From remaining white broadcloth, cut approximately 60 inches of 1½-inch-wide bias. Encase the outer edges with bias. Fold the tieback in half; sew a ring to two corners, joining them.

Repeat instructions to make a second tieback.

Chair Pad Set

Shown on page 50.

Finished chair pads, excluding ruffles, are approximately 14x15 inches.

MATERIALS
2 yards of lavender print fabric
½ yard *each* of white fabric and white sheer fabric
Scraps of lavender, black, and pink fabrics and dark lavender print fabric
Paper-backed fusible webbing
15x16-inch piece of polyester batting
Large tapestry needle
Polyester fiberfill
Lavender embroidery floss
Tailor's chalk pencils
Tracing paper

INSTRUCTIONS
Trace the girl pattern on page 58. The dashed lines on the patterns indicate where pieces are partially covered by other shapes. The blue lines indicate quilting and embroidery lines.

On a large sheet of paper, draw a 9½x12½-inch oval; cut out the oval to use as a pattern.

From the lavender print fabric, cut four 14½x15½-inch rectangles for the pillow fronts and the pillow backs. Cut six 4½x44-inch strips for the ruffles and six 2x44-inch strips for the ties.

Cut one 14½x15½-inch rectangle *each* from the white and sheer fabrics for the oval insert on the back pad.

From the white fabric, cut one 15x16-inch rectangle for the back pad lining.

To make the back pad
TO MAKE PILLOW TOP: Using tailor's chalk, draw the outline of the oval on the white fabric rectangle and on the *right* side of one lavender rectangle.

Referring to the Shadow Appliqué instructions on page 52, prepare and cut the appliqué pieces for one girl from assorted fabric scraps. Patterns are finished size; *do not* add seam allowances when cutting fabric pieces.

Using the traced pattern, draw placement guides within the oval on the white fabric. Working from the background to the foreground, fuse the appliqués within guidelines.

Using your choice of floss and stitches, embroider details such as a hat band and flowers.

Cover the block with sheer fabric. Baste around the perimeter to secure the layers.

Cut out the oval from the lavender rectangle, leaving ¼-inch seams to the inside of the line. Turn under and baste the seam allowance around the oval.

Appliqué around the lavender oval to attach it to the white fabrics. Leaving ¼-inch seam allowances, trim the excess white and sheer fabric from behind the lavender fabric.

Layer the batting, white lining rectangle, and pillow top; baste.

Outline-quilt around the appliqué pieces, adding additional quilting as desired.

FINISHING: Sew three ruffle strips together to form a loop. Press ruffle in half, lengthwise, with wrong sides facing. Gather and baste one-fourth of ruffle to each side of pillow front.

With right sides facing, pin the the pillow front atop a lavender
continued

HEN

CAT

LAMB

GIRL

Full-Size Patterns

Full-Size Patterns

rectangle. Sew around the pillow, leaving an opening for turning. Clip, turn, lightly stuff, and stitch the opening closed.

To make one tie, fold a 2-inch-wide lavender strip in half lengthwise with right sides facing. Stitch around the tie, leaving an opening for turning. Clip, turn, and stitch the opening closed. Edge-stitch around the tie.

Sew a tie to one corner of the pad. Repeat to make and attach three more ties.

To make the chair pad

Following the finishing instructions for back pad, sew the chair pad, omitting the appliqué and the quilting.

Referring to the instructions for the ties for the back pad, make ties from the remaining 2½-inch-wide lavender strips. Attach ties to the two back corners.

Using a tapestry needle threaded with six strands of lavender embroidery floss, tie the layers of the chair pad approximately every 3 to 4 inches to keep the polyester fiberfill from shifting.

Child's Dress

Shown on page 54.

MATERIALS
⅜ yard *each* of white fabric and
    white sheer fabric
Scraps of lavender, lavender
    print, and dark green fabrics
    for the appliqués
Commercial dress pattern, such
    as Simplicity 8522
Fabric and notions as listed on
    the pattern
Paper-backed fusible webbing
Tailor's chalk pencils
Tracing paper

INSTRUCTIONS

Using the collar patterns included in the dress pattern, cut one collar back and two collar fronts *each* from the white broadcloth and the sheer fabric.

From the lavender print fabric, cut the other dress pieces as instructed in the pattern.

Trace the pansy and leaf pattern, *opposite.*

Referring to the Shadow Appliqué instructions on page 52, prepare and cut the pieces for five pansies and 10 leaves. The patterns are finished size; *do not* add seam allowances when cutting the pieces from the fabrics.

From the lavender print fabric, cut five pansies. Cut five centers from the lavender fabric. Cut 10 leaves from the dark green fabric.

Using the traced pattern and a tailor's chalk pencil, draw placement guidelines on the broadcloth collar pieces. Position one pansy and two leaves along the lower edge of each collar front. Position three pansies and six leaves along the lower collar back, placing a pansy in the center and in each corner.

Working from background to foreground, fuse the leaves and pansies within the corresponding placement guidelines. Fuse a center atop each pansy.

Cover each collar piece with matching sheer fabric piece. Baste around the outer edges. Outline-quilt around the appliqué shapes.

Treating each of the layered collar pieces as one, construct collar and dress according to the pattern instructions.

Baby Bib

Shown on page 55.

Finished bib is approximately 12x14 inches.

MATERIALS
½ yard *each* of white
    broadcloth fabric, lavender
    print fabric, and white sheer
    fabric
Scraps of pink and lavender
    print fabrics and green,
    lavender, and black fabrics
Paper-backed fusible webbing
Black embroidery floss
13x15-inch piece of polyester
    batting
Tailor's chalk pencils
Tracing paper

INSTRUCTIONS

Enlarge the bib pattern, *opposite.* Trace tulip and butterfly patterns, *opposite,* on tracing paper.

Cut one bib *each* from the batting and the white, lavender print, and sheer fabrics.

Referring to the Shadow Appliqué instructions on page 52, prepare and cut the pieces for the appliqués. The patterns are finished size; *do not* add seam allowances when cutting the appliqué pieces from the fabrics.

From the pink print fabric, cut one butterfly.

From the black fabric, cut one butterfly body.

From the green fabric, cut one tulip leaf and one stem.

From the lavender fabric, cut one tulip tip.

From the lavender print fabric, cut one tulip.

Using a chalk pencil and the traced patterns, draw placement guidelines for appliqué pieces; fuse pieces within the guidelines.

Using a chalk pencil, draw antennae on the butterfly. Using black embroidery floss, embroider the butterfly antennae in outline stitch.

Place the sheer fabric atop the bib; baste around the perimeter.

Layer the bib, batting, and lavender print bib back; baste the three layers together.

Outline-quilt close to all appliqué pieces. Add additional quilting as desired.

From the remaining lavender print fabric, cut approximately 2¼ yards of 1½-inch-wide bias.

With right sides facing and raw edges matching, sew bias around the outside of the bib. Turn under ¼ inch along the raw edge; bring the fold to bib back. Blindstitch the folded edge to the bib back.

In a similar manner, sew bias to the neck edge, leaving approximately 12 to 15 inches extending on each end for the ties.

Turn the raw edge of the ties to the center; fold ties in half. Machine-topstitch along the ties and around the neckline.

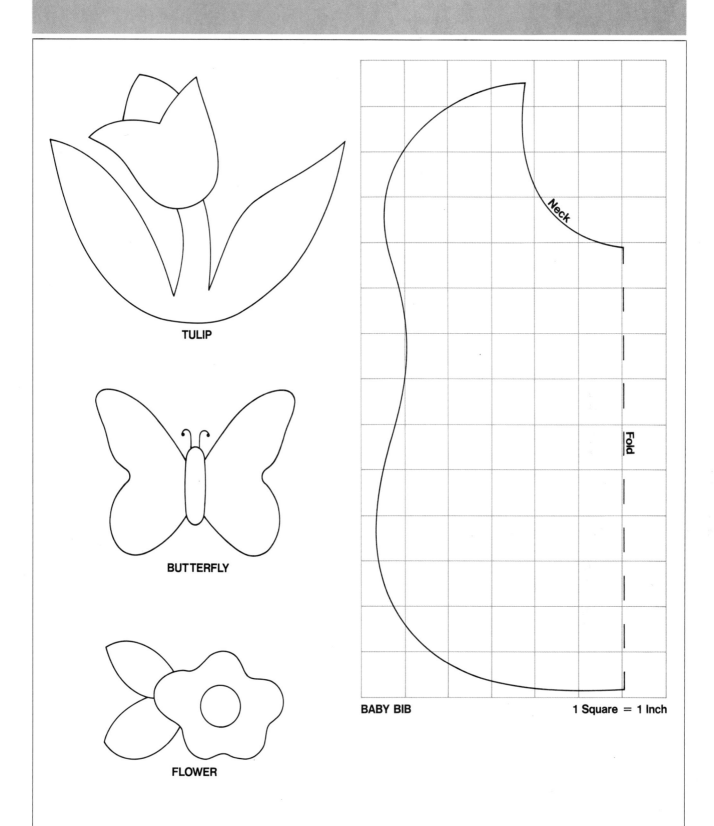

TULIP

BUTTERFLY

FLOWER

Neck

Fold

BABY BIB

1 Square = 1 Inch

ENGLISH GARDEN

BRODERIE PERSE

♦ ♦ ♦

Because there were high tariffs on imported chintz, 18th-century British needlewomen used *broderie perse*, Persian embroidery, to stretch one yard of chintz to embellish an entire quilt. We used this elegant stitchery method to create the fabric floral arrangement on this wall hanging, *opposite.*

1 Using embroidery scissors or other small, sharp scissors, cut leaves, flowers, and other desired motifs from cotton chintz fabric. Cut a generous ⅛ inch beyond the design outline to allow for seam allowances.

When cutting the pieces, cut away any narrow stems, tendrils, and other detail lines that surround a shape because they are difficult to appliqué and will not read well in the finished project.

Cut large clusters of flowers into individual flowers so you can rearrange the individual blooms.

Cutouts from a variety of other fabrics can be combined in the same project if the colors and motifs are compatible.

Glazed cotton chintz is the traditional and most popular fabric to use for the cutouts because it is tightly woven and does not fray easily. If you use fabrics that tend to fray, fuse lightweight fusible interfacing to the wrong side of the fabrics before cutting the pieces, or treat the edges of cutouts with a commercial fray preventer or clear nail polish.

2 Arrange the cutouts on the background fabric to plan your design. Leaves, flowers, and other shapes can be spread out more than on the original fabric, or overlapped.

When you are pleased with the design, pin or baste the cutouts to the background fabric.

3 Using embroidery floss that coordinates with each cutout, buttonhole-stitch the cutouts to the background fabric. As you stitch, use the needle tip to roll under the seam allowance just ahead of where you are stitching.

If desired, add additional embroidery in stitches of your choice to embellish the design.

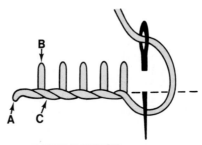

BUTTONHOLE STITCH

Broderie Perse Wall Hanging

Shown on pages 63 and 65.

Finished wall hanging is 22x27 inches.

MATERIALS
1 yard of tan fabric
½ yard or a minimum of one pattern repeat of floral cotton chintz fabric
¾ yard of polyester batting
½ yard *each* of dark and medium brown fabrics
One package of dark green bias quilt binding
Embroidery floss to coordinate with the chintz motifs
Water-erasable marking pen

INSTRUCTIONS
Note: These instructions are written to make a project similar to the wall hanging *above*. Adapt them as needed to make a wall hanging that features the motifs printed on your piece of chintz to their best advantage.

TO MAKE THE BASKET: For the background, cut one 22x27-inch rectangle from the tan fabric. Repeat to cut the project back.

Enlarge the basket pattern *below*, completing the half pattern.

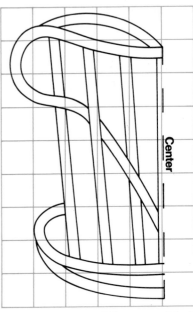

1 Square = 1 Inch

Using a water-erasable marking pen, trace the basket outline onto the background fabric, flopping the design to complete the basket.

Referring to the instructions for bias appliqué on page 28, prepare ¼-inch-wide bias strips for the basket from the medium and dark brown fabrics.

Baste the bias strips along the basket outline, weaving the strips as shown on the pattern and in the project photographs.

TO MAKE FLORAL ARRANGE-MENT: Referring to the instructions for broderie perse, *opposite,* cut an assortment of flowers and leaves from the chintz fabric.

Position the cutouts above the basket, allowing some flowers and leaves to overlap the top of the basket. Experiment with various arrangements of the flowers and leaves until you have a pleasing design. Pin or baste cutouts to the background fabric.

Using embroidery floss in colors that match or accentuate the cutouts, appliqué the flowers and leaves to the background using a buttonhole stitch.

Using regular sewing thread, appliqué the bias strips.

FINISHING: Referring to the project photographs for inspiration, use a water-erasable pen to draw quilting designs in each corner of the wall hanging. Mark additional quilting lines as desired.

Layer the project back, batting, and appliquéd piece; baste. Outline-quilt around the bias strips and chintz cutouts. Quilt the quilting designs.

Bind the outer edges with green bias binding.

To make a hanging sleeve, cut a 6x25-inch piece from the remaining tan fabric. Press under ¼ inch on both short ends of the tan piece; press under another ¼ inch and hem. Press ½ inch to the wrong side on both long edges.

Center the prepared sleeve on the back of the wall hanging, approximately 1 inch below the top edge. Blindstitch the sleeve to the project back, making sure the stitching does not show on the project front.

TRAPUNTO QUILTING

♦ ♦ ♦

Ask any group of quilters what the most exquisite variation of quilting is, and the chances are that they will answer "trapunto." Worked on lightly colored or white fabrics, each tiny quilting stitch shows to perfection. Extra stuffing within the quilted areas gives the designs added dimension. Here and on the following pages is a sampling of projects that are made with this elegant technique.

Doves, symbols of love and devotion, are framed by interlocking rings on the ringbearer's pillow *opposite*. Trim the pillow with piping and a ruffle in fabric that matches the bridesmaids' dresses. Choose a coordinating color of satin ribbon to trim the doves and to secure the wedding rings.

To preserve memories of the special day, stitch a special album for the wedding photographs. Embroider the names of the wedding couple and the date with pastel embroidery floss, and stuff the contours of the feathered heart design with colored yarn.

Instructions for these and the other projects in this chapter begin on page 74.

TRAPUNTO QUILTING

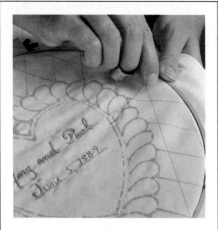

1 Using a water-erasable pen, trace the heart design on page 75 onto one fabric rectangle. Write the names and marriage date in the heart. Using a ruler, mark the background around the heart with a diagonally set grid of 1-inch squares.

Outline-stitch the names and the date with embroidery floss.

With wrong sides facing, baste the marked rectangle atop a second rectangle.

Quilt the heart design.

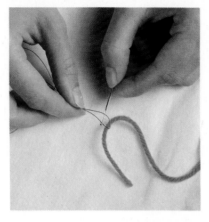

2 Thread a large tapestry needle with yarn. Adjust the yarn so the tails are even.

To easily thread a needle with yarn, make your own needle threader with a length of heavy thread, such as quilting thread. Fold the thread in half; insert the folded portion through the needle eye. Slip the end of the yarn into the thread loop. Pull the thread back through the eye of the needle, pulling the yarn through the needle eye.

Trapunto Methods

Traditionally, quilters have used two basic trapunto techniques to raise design areas and add extra dimension to quilted projects.

Corded quilting, also called Italian quilting, refers to the process of filling quilted outlines with yarn or soft cord. In shadow quilting, a variation of corded quilting, colored yarn is worked into the quilted areas. When colored yarn is used with relatively sheer white fabric, the colored yarn shows through, resulting in softly colored, dimensional designs. The method for doing corded shadow quilting is described at *left*.

Filling relatively large design areas, such as the dove bodies on the Dove Pillow, shown on page 66, becomes very time consuming and tedious with the cording method. To fill large areas like these more easily and quickly, use the method commonly called stuffed quilting or stuffed work.

After the project has been quilted, cut a small slit through the backing fabric in the center of the area to be stuffed. Be careful not to cut the top fabric. Insert scraps of batting or polyester fiberfill through the opening, using a blunt instrument such as a small crochet hook or knitting needle to distribute the stuffing evenly and to work the stuffing into the small detail areas. Work with small amounts of filling at one time to help avoid creating lumps. Be careful not to overstuff and distort the design.

After the areas have been filled, bring the cut edges together without overlapping them. If the design is distorted, remove some of the stuffing. When you are satisfied with the results, stitch the cut edges together with large, loose cross-stitches.

Projects made with the stuffed quilting method should be lined to protect and cover the slit backing fabric.

3 Working from the *back* side, insert the needle into one section of the quilted design and come out on the other side. Pull the yarn into the quilted area; clip the yarn, leaving short tails that are approximately ½ inch long. Repeat until the area is padded evenly with yarn.

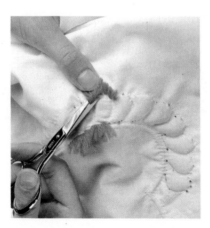

4 After you have filled several areas with yarn, use small embroidery scissors to carefully clip ends of the yarn close to the fabric surface.

Delicate pastel daisies and leaves trail along opposite corners of this softly padded frame, *above.* You'll want to use brightly colored yarns to stuff the flower centers, leaves, and stems because the color intensities of the yarns will diminish when they are placed between the layers of fabrics.

Six seashells, arranged around a sand dollar, create a starlike design on the collar *opposite.* Two shells, with the narrow ends pointing outward, decorate the belt.

TRAPUNTO QUILTING

elebrate the traditional southern symbol of springtime by decorating the insets on a nightgown and coordinating cosmetic bag with strings of dogwood blossoms.

The nightgown, *opposite,* fashioned in lightweight pale green batiste, will be cool and comfortable to wear as the evenings grow warmer.

Stitch the gown using a commercial garment pattern, or add the trapunto bands to a purchased gown cut in a similar style.

The barrel-shaped cosmetics bag, *near right,* is roomy enough to tote all your cosmetics and toiletry items.

Stitch the bag from a tiny plaid or check that matches your nightwear. For embellishments, accent the trapunto design with pink ribbon, and use piping around the ends of the bag to help the bag hold its shape.

Instructions for the cosmetics bag and nightgown begin on page 78.

Ring Bearer's Pillow

Shown on page 66.

Finished pillow is approximately 8x11 inches.

MATERIALS
½ yard of white satin fabric
½ yard of mauve and cream print fabric
¼ yard of white batiste fabric
1 yard of mauve ¼-inch-wide ribbon
½ yard of cord for piping
White quilting thread
½ yard of polyester fleece
Polyester fiberfill; tracing paper
Water-erasable marking pen
Large tapestry needle
White polyester yarn

INSTRUCTIONS

Trace the dove pattern, *below,* onto tracing paper, expanding the half-pattern to the full pattern. The small diagram to the right of the pattern shows the complete design.

From the satin fabric, cut two 8½x11½-inch rectangles for the pillow front and back.

From the fleece, cut one 8½x11½-inch rectangle to line the pillow front.

For the oval front design, cut one 9x13-inch rectangle *each* from the satin, the batiste, and the polyester fleece.

Using a water-erasable marking pen or other removable marker, trace the dove quilting design, including the oval indicated with a blue line, onto the satin fabric.

Layer the 9x13-inch batiste, fleece, and satin ovals, placing the satin rectangle on top. Baste the layers together.

Quilt the dove and rings design. Do not quilt the blue oval line.

Referring to the trapunto instructions on page 68, cord doves' feathers and the rings around the doves with white yarn. Slit the backing fabric at the center of each dove body. Stuff the bodies lightly with fiberfill; stitch the openings closed.

To make the piping, cover the cable cord with cream and pink print fabric. Baste piping around the oval along the line indicated in blue on the pattern.

Cut out the oval, adding ¼-inch seam allowances.

Turn under the seam allowance around the oval along the piping. Using a zipper foot and matching thread, machine-topstitch the oval to the pillow front.

Baste the fleece to the wrong side of the pillow front.

For the ruffle, cut two 2½x45-inch strips from the cream and pink print fabric. Sew the strips together into a tube. Fold the ruffle in half with wrong sides facing so it is 1¼ inches wide. Run a gathering thread around the ruffle along the seam line. Baste the ruffle to the pillow front, gathering the ruffle to fit.

With right sides facing, sew the pillow front to the pillow back, leaving an opening for turning. Clip, turn, and stuff with fiberfill. Stitch the opening closed.

Cut two 9-inch pieces and one 18-inch piece of ribbon. Tie each short ribbon into a small bow. Tack a bow at the neck of each dove. Tack the center of the 18-inch ribbon at the lower intersection of the rings. Thread wedding rings onto the ribbon, and tie the ribbon into a bow.

RING BEARER'S PILLOW

FEATHERED HEART FOR PHOTOGRAPH ALBUM

Feathered-Heart Photograph Album

Shown on pages 67–69.

The finished photograph album is 10¾x11½ inches.

MATERIALS
2 yards of white batiste fabric
½ yard of polyester fleece
¼ yard of pink and cream print fabric
Pink polyester yarn
Large tapestry needle
Pink embroidery floss
Water-erasable marking pen
Tracing paper
3 yards of cord for piping
Purchased photograph album, approximately 10¾x11½ inches

INSTRUCTIONS
Note: The instructions are written to custom-cover any album of similar size.

Trace the feathered-heart design on page 75.

To make the album cover patterns, draw two rectangles onto brown paper. Draw one the size of the album front cover and the second the size of the spine. To make the pattern for the inner flaps, draw a rectangle as long as the front cover pattern but only 8 inches wide. Add ½-inch seam allowances to the patterns.

To make the design panel
From the white batiste fabric, cut three large rectangles for the album front, front facing, and front lining, cutting the fabric approximately 1 inch larger all around than the pattern. Cut a matching piece from fleece.

Referring to the instructions on page 68, embroider the names and date. Quilt the heart design on the front panel; stuff the heart design with pink yarn.

Layer the front panel, the fleece, and the front lining piece; baste. Quilt the grid design.

When the quilting is complete, use the front cover pattern to mark the size of the front cover. Baste around the cover just inside the line. Trim the cover to size.

To make the album cover
From the batiste, cut one back cover, one spine, and two flaps.

Cut matching pieces from the fleece. Baste fleece pieces to the wrong side of the back cover, spine and two flaps.

FINISHING: From cream and pink print fabric, cut 1-inch-wide strips to cover the cord. Join the fabric strips. To make the piping, fold the fabric over the cord; baste, using a zipper foot.

Sew piping to *each* long edge of the spine piece. With right sides facing, sew the front and back covers to the spine. Trim seams to ¼ inch. Sew piping atop the seam line around all sides, right sides facing. Trim the seam allowance to ¼ inch.

Using the assembled cover as a pattern, cut a lining from batiste to match.

On one long side of *each* inner flap piece, press under ½ inch twice; machine-stitch hem. With right sides facing and raw edges even, sew the flaps to the ends of the cover.

Pin the right side of the lining atop the wrong side of the flaps. Sew the lining, through all thicknesses, atop the cover, leaving an opening for turning. Clip corners, turn right side out, and press. Sew the opening closed.

Slip the flaps over the album.

Shell Collar and Belt

Shown on page 71.

MATERIALS
1 yard of peach fabric
White polyester yarn
Large tapestry needle
Tracing paper
Water-erasable marking pen
¾ yard of white batiste fabric
2 yards *each* of peach lace and piping
Purchased collar pattern
Notions as specified on collar pattern
¼ yard of fusible interfacing
Self-grip fastening tape or skirt hook and eye fasteners

INSTRUCTIONS
Trace the Shell Design, *opposite,* onto tracing paper.

To make the collar
Referring to the cutting instructions for the collar pattern, cut the collar front, back, and matching lining pieces from the peach fabric.

For the interfacing, cut one collar front from the batiste.

Using a water-erasable marking pen, trace the shell design on the collar front.

Baste the batiste interfacing to the wrong side of the collar front. Quilt the shell design.

Referring to the instructions on page 68, stuff the quilted shapes with yarn.

Sew the shoulder seams as directed in the pattern instructions. Baste piping and lace around the neck opening and the outer edge of the collar.

Finish the collar as directed in the pattern instructions.

To make the belt
From the peach fabric, cut two 3-inch-wide pieces the size of your waist measurement plus approximately 5 inches for overlap. Measurements include ¼ inch for seam allowances.

Cut one matching piece *each* from the fusible interfacing and the batiste.

Fold one peach piece in half *widthwise* to find the center. Using a water-erasable pen, draw one shell approximately ½ inch from *each* side of the center, with the widest part of the shells at the center of the belt.

Baste the batiste piece to the wrong side of the marked piece.

Quilt the shell design. Referring to the instructions on page 68, stuff the design with yarn, working from the back side.

Fuse interfacing to the wrong side of the unmarked peach piece.

With right sides facing, sew belt to lining, leaving an opening for turning. Clip, turn, and press. Using matching thread, machine-topstitch along the seams and ¼ inch from the seams.

Try on belt. Mark positions for fasteners; sew fasteners to belt.

SHELL DESIGN

Daisy Frame

Shown on page 70.

The frame is 8x10 inches.

MATERIALS
½ yard of cream batiste fabric
Polyester yarn in the following
    colors: white, bright yellow,
    and bright green
Large tapestry needle
1¼ yards of lace
One package of yellow piping
Two pieces of cardboard, each
    8x10 inches
8x10-inch piece of 1-inch-thick
    polyester batting
White quilting thread
Mat knife
Water-erasable marking pen
Masking tape
Crafts glue or hot-glue gun and
    glue sticks

DAISY DESIGN

INSTRUCTIONS
From the cream batiste fabric,
cut four 10x12-inch rectangles.
Trace the Daisy Design, *below,*
onto tracing paper.

FOR FRAME FRONT: Using a
mat knife, cut a 4¼x6¼-inch
rectangle from the center of one
cardboard piece.
To mark the front fabric, use a
water-erasable marker to draw
the frame outline on one fabric
piece. Referring to the photograph on page 70, draw the daisy
design in the lower left corner and
in the upper right corner of the
frame fabric.
Layer the front fabric and an
unmarked fabric piece. Baste
around the outer edge. Quilt the
daisy designs.
Referring to the instructions on
page 68, stuff the stems and the
leaves with the green yarn. Stuff
the daisy centers with the yellow
yarn; stuff the petals with the
white yarn.
Baste piping to the frame front
along the center opening line and
around the frame outline. To line
the front, pin a fabric piece to the
frame front, with right sides facing. Sew around the center opening atop the piping. Slit the center
from corner to corner diagonally
and trim the excess fabric from
the opening. To turn the frame
right side out, pull the fabric
through the opening.
Glue the batting to the cardboard frame, trimming the batting from the center opening.
Slip the padded cardboard between the frame front and the lining, keeping the lining at the
frame back and pulling the quilted fabric through the opening to
the frame front. Secure the lining
to the frame back with tape and
glue, making sure center seams
are aligned with frame opening.
Stretch the fabric over the
frame front, pulling outer edges
to the frame back. Make sure the
fabric is smooth and the piping is
aligned with the frame edge. Tape
and glue the fabric edges to the
frame back.
Glue lace around the outside of
the frame.

FINISHING: To make the frame
back, cut the remaining cardboard slightly smaller than the
frame. Cover the back of the cardboard with a fabric piece, pulling
the edges to the other side. Secure
fabric edges with tape and glue.
Tape a photograph or picture to
the uncovered side of the frame
back so it will appear in the opening. Whipstitch the frame back to
the frame front.

Nightgown

Shown on pages 72 and 73.

MATERIALS
¼ yard of white batiste fabric
Purchased nightgown pattern
    (we used Butterick 3778)
Dark pink, brown, and green
    polyester yarn
Large tapestry needle
Mint green batiste fabric and
    notions as listed on the
    garment pattern
2½ yards of ¼-inch-wide
    mint green ribbon
Tracing paper
Water-erasable marking pen

INSTRUCTIONS
Trace the Dogwood Design, *opposite,* onto tracing paper.
From the white batiste, cut two
3x10-inch rectangles for the design panels.
Using a water-erasable marker,
trace the dogwood pattern onto
each rectangle, reversing the design for the second rectangle.

Pin the marked rectangles atop the remaining white batiste fabric; baste around the outer edges.

Quilt the dogwood design. Referring to the trapunto instructions on page 68, stuff the leaves and flower centers with green yarn. Stuff the stems and petal tips with brown yarn. Stuff the petals with pink yarn.

Cut out the panel pieces. Pin a panel on each gown front along the positions indicated for the lace insert. Topstitch ribbon atop the raw edges of the panel.

Construct the gown as directed in the pattern instructions. Cut a length of ribbon and tack a bow to the top of the front neck.

Cosmetics Bag

Shown on page 72.

Finished bag is approximately 8½ inches long.

MATERIALS
½ yard of white and green plaid fabric
½ yard of white fabric
⅛ yard of white batiste fabric
1 yard of ¼-inch-wide pink ribbon
Green, brown, and dark pink yarn
9x18-inch piece of polyester batting or fleece
9-inch skirt zipper
Pink piping
Tracing paper
Drafting compass
Water-erasable marking pen
Large tapestry needle

INSTRUCTIONS
Trace the Dogwood Design, *right,* onto tracing paper.

Using a compass, draw a 5-inch-diameter circle on paper to make the pattern for the ends of the bag. Cut out the pattern. The measurements for the patterns include ¼-inch seam allowances.

TO MAKE DESIGN PANEL: From the white batiste fabric, cut one 2½x9-inch rectangle. Using a water-erasable pen, draw the dogwood design on the rectangle. Pin the rectangle atop the remaining batiste; baste around the perimeter. Quilt the dogwood design.

Referring to the trapunto instructions on page 68, stuff the leaves and the flower centers with green yarn. Stuff the stems and petal tips with brown yarn. Stuff the petals with pink yarn. Cut out the panel.

TO MAKE BAG: Cut one 9x18-inch rectangle *each* from plaid fabric, white fabric, and fleece.

Using the circular bag-end pattern, cut two *each* from plaid fabric, white fabric, and fleece.

Layer the rectangles with fleece between the pieces. Machine-quilt along the lines of the plaid, spacing quilting lines approximately 1 inch apart. Repeat to machine-quilt the bag ends.

Pin the design panel atop the quilted rectangle, approximately 2½ inches from one end. Using matching thread, topstitch a ribbon piece atop the raw edges of the panel.

Baste piping along the two long edges of the bag rectangle.

Trim the zipper to length, and insert the zipper between the two short edges of the rectangle, forming a tube.

Sew a bag end to one end of the bag, easing as necessary. Repeat for the other bag end.

From the remaining plaid fabric, cut one 2½-inch-wide strip across the fabric width for the handles. Fold strip in half lengthwise; stitch along the long edge. Turn strip right side out; press so the seam is centered on one side. Topstitch along both long sides. Cut the strip into two 22-inch-long pieces.

Stitch handles to the bag.

DOGWOOD DESIGN FOR THE NIGHTGOWN AND COSMETICS BAG

ACKNOWLEDGMENTS

We would like to extend our special thanks to the following designers who contributed projects to this book. When more than one project appears on a page, the acknowledgment cites both the project and the page number. A page number alone indicates that the one designer contributed all of the projects on that page.

Kris Cable—26-27

Dorothy Crowdes—50-51, 53-55

Karan Flanscha—30-31

Bettina Havig—66; 70-71; 73, nightgown

Kathleen Niklas Herman—62-63, 65

Ilene Kagarice and Martha Street—72, cosmetics bag

Kris Kerrigan—4-5, 7

Liz Porter—10-11; 67 and 69, album

Martha Street and Ilene Kagarice—72, cosmetics bag

Joan DuBay Tully—8-9, 32-35

A special thank-you to the following people, who loaned us quilts or projects:

Carita Kelleher—46-47

Robin Ventner—31, framed tulips

We would like to thank the following people, whose technical skills are greatly appreciated.

Ilene Kagarice

Martha Street

For their cooperation and courtesy, we extend a special thanks to the following sources:

Omnigrid
15806 Highway 99 No. 4
Lynnwood, WA 98037
  for rulers

Wamsutta-Pacific Home Products
1285 Avenue of the Americas
New York, NY 10019
  for bed linens on page 11

We also are pleased to acknowledge the photographers whose talents and technical skills contributed much to this book.

Hopkins Associates—6-7, 22-25,28-30, 34-35, 46-47, 50-55,64-69

Scott Little—8-11, 26-27, 31-33, 62-63, 70-73

Perry Struse—4-5

Have BETTER HOMES AND GARDENS® magazine delivered to your door. For information, write to:
MR. ROBERT AUSTIN
P.O. BOX 4536
DES MOINES, IA 50336